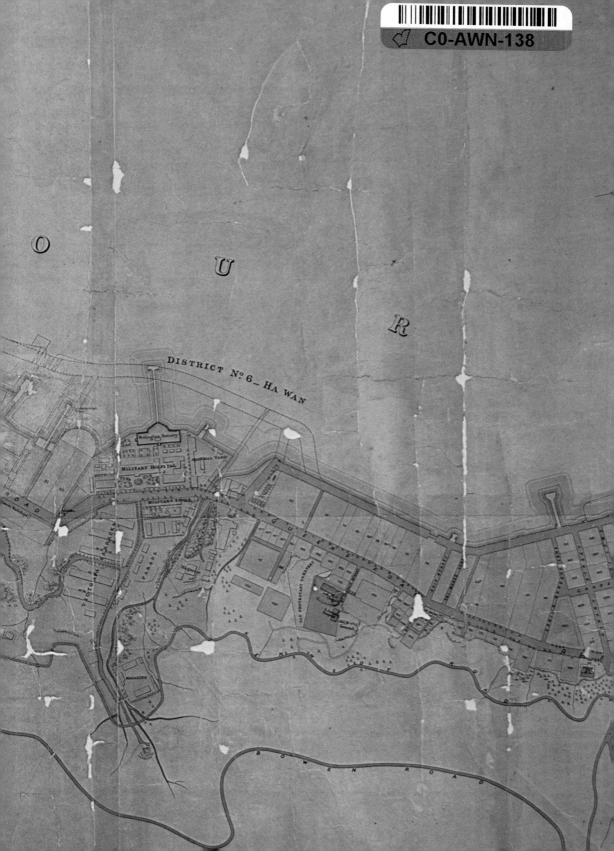

O
U
R

DISTRICT Nº 6 – HA WAN

Government House, Upper Albert Road

1850

1900

1950

This is Hong Kong:
The Story of Government House

by Katherine Mattock

A Hong Kong Government Publication

First published January 1978

 Produced by Government Information Services

Printed by the Government Printer

Contents

Assistance from Hong Kong University Press and the Public Records Office, Hong Kong, is gratefully acknowledged.
Particular thanks are also due to Major-General Sir Robert Neville, Seichi Fujimura, Kinya Nakao, Wendy Harris, Frank Eckermann and Dr Alan Birch.

The plan

TEN years after Hong Kong was formally declared a British colony, a man by the name of Charles St George Cleverly was trying to build a mansion overlooking its harbour.

Things were not going well for him. The contractor was on the verge of bankruptcy and paying no attention to his job. The masons had gone on strike because they were owed money, so that Cleverly had been obliged to guarantee to pay them himself. The whole project was behind schedule.

Two years later the house was still unfinished 'notwithstanding,' lamented Cleverly, 'I have made every possible exertion to expedite the work'. The contractor continued to be dilatory. Pirates had held up supplies and the Chinese on the Kowloon shore had demanded exorbitant prices for lime. There was no one who could tackle the plumbing or bell-hanging without Cleverly's personal supervision. And he himself had had fever, he said, through carelessness in exposing himself to the sun and because 'during my service of nearly 12 years in this climate, I have never obtained leave of absence to England and but once for a period of six weeks to Shanghae; and thus it is perhaps surprising that I should have had such equable health or have been so seldom unable to do my work . . .'

The man who fretted about himself and his work at such length was Hong Kong's second and longest-serving Surveyor General. The house he was trying to build, and to the design of which he put his name, was Government House on Upper Albert Road.

Temporary solutions

BEHIND Cleverly's frustration stood a decade of delays and delaying tactics.

Possession of the island had been taken by Captain Elliot in January 1841 and in June of 1841, from Macau, Elliot had charged his deputy A. R. Johnston with the government of it. But it was two more years before Hong Kong was officially erected into a British colony and a Governor proper could be appointed.

Even then, the British were not sure they had done the right thing. Pottinger, that first official Governor, and the three men who succeeded him, were out of Hong Kong as much as they were in it, fighting China for a better deal; and whenever the going (or the trading) was rough, people were liable to list the island's disadvantages and say, for example, how much better a base Chusan would have made, further up the coast. The colony's future frequently seemed in the balance. The last thing for which its preoccupied merchants or the cynical local press or the increasingly cautious Colonial Office men back in England were likely to push was a prestigious Government House.

Cleverly's house, under matshed

The early governors consequently had to shift for a home and Johnston's first residence on the island, arguably the first Government House of all, was so flimsy it was blown down in a typhoon four weeks after Elliot put him in charge.

Pottinger, when he took over from Elliot in August 1841 as Plenipotentiary, Superintendent of Trade and *de facto* Governor of Hong Kong, anchored in the bay overnight on his way north to fight and was not seen there again for six months. When he did return, he had to live in an office, newly constructed on the hill above the bay and facetiously described by the *Canton Press* as 'so inconveniently sited on a steep ascent that an ardent inquirer must, to arrive there, expose himself to the risk of solar martyrdom'.

This 'Record Office' combined the functions of Governor's residence, Governor's office and general government offices. On June 26, 1843, extended by two bungalows, it even served to receive China's Imperial Commissioner Keying at the formal ceremonies marking the cession of Hong Kong.

But Pottinger, now Governor in name as well as in practice, took over for government use a house on a small bluff at the top of Battery Path; and Davis, when he succeeded Pottinger in 1844, decided to live in Johnston's house rather than up the hill at the Record Office. Then, early in 1846, disturbed by its proximity to the drums and bugles of the parade ground, he moved back uphill to a new house built by the Magistrate, Caine.

Bonham, succeeding Davis in 1848, moved himself and his family east, beyond the whole government/military area, to a house on the waterfront at Spring Gardens. Bowring, coming after him, also lived at Spring Gardens.

So Hong Kong's first governors shuffled between temporary government quarters and rented mansions, often living in one place and having their office in another, with the name 'Government House' being loosely attached to either building or both.

From the start, however, whether merchants or press or Colonial Office wanted one or not, those governors planned for a Government House proper and planned for it to be where Cleverly eventually built it and where it stands today. The Record Office on 'Government Hill' was in today's Botanical Gardens; and as early as May 1842 Pottinger was cautioning Johnston that his proposed house on the bluff must 'not interfere with the site that may hereafter be required – should Hong Kong become a British colony – for the Government House and its premises, which it appears to me will be in front of the buildings erected as an office and Record Office and in which I am now residing'.

In subsequent correspondence, Pottinger earmarked Government Hill for a church and all major public offices. The military canton-

Johnston's house on the bluff.

ment was to keep to the east of the new barracks going up and land was to be reclaimed directly in front of the hill for use as an open, tree-lined space. By 1844, Pottinger was calling it 'Government House Hill'.

His plan in its essentials was accepted. Governor Davis did say at one stage that he would prefer not to proceed with a permanent Government House until it had been established that the north side of the island was not the unhealthy side; and six years later Governor Bonham wearily suggested that, if the services of a General Officer Commanding were dispensed with, *his* house might be converted into a suitable residence for the Governor. But these were the only official hesitations about the actual siting of Government House, and neither was expressed again.

Production of a master-plan was one thing. Putting that plan into effect in its entirety proved to be quite another. By the end of 1848, Government Hill had a substantial new block of Government Offices. By mid-1849, it had St John's Cathedral. But higher up, in front of the old Record Office, the site for a Government House stood empty. By the time Cleverly was allowed to start construction, Lord Palmerston's 'barren island with hardly a house upon it' was a city of more than 30,000 people. By the time Cleverly finished, the total had passed 70,000.

1

Record Office
on Government Hill (1841-44)

Hong Kong's first official Governor did not force the issue of a permanent Government House. He knew where he wanted it to be but there were many more pressing problems and he obviously never contemplated construction of it during his hectic tenure.

Sir Henry Pottinger arrived at Macau in August 1841, to take over from Captain Elliot as Her Majesty's Plenipotentiary and Chief Superintendent of Trade. After ten days' residence at the Chief Superintendent's office there, he left for the north aboard the *Queen* to pursue hostilities with China, landing only briefly on the way at Hong Kong 'in the evening and also the next morning' to observe the progress of the public works.[1] Like Elliot before him, he left Deputy Superintendent A. R. Johnston in charge of the government of the island.

Pottinger stayed with the expedition until 1842. Returning from it on the *Blenheim* in February, he caught up with developments in Hong Kong from aboard ship and proceeded to Macau.

At the end of the month, he transferred his headquarters from the old Portuguese settlement to the new British one, moving into part of a Record Office that Johnston had had built on Government Hill 'to serve as a temporary residence for the head of the government'.[2] From March 1842, Pottinger's Hong Kong correspondence was headed 'Government House'.

It sounded impressive but clearly was not. The whole complex cost less than $8,000 to build and after a year of its being used as residence, offices and even church when weddings had to be performed, Pottinger needed something a little better.[3]

'In consequence of the very limited accommodation of the building at present called Government House and the advisability of deferring the erection of a more suitable one until some definite plans for the public buildings can be laid down,' wrote Pottinger's Private Secretary Richard Woosnam to Land Officer A. T. Gordon in April 1843, 'I am directed by Sir Henry Pottinger to request that you will be good enough to prepare plans and estimates for buildings of the following description, bearing in mind that they are to be of a temporary nature: one bungalow consisting of three rooms, as dining-room, breakfast-room and receiving-room; another bungalow consisting of four moderate-sized rooms as bedrooms . . .'[4]

One month later, for Pottinger's investiture as Knight Grand Cross, 'a throne was erected in the reception-room of the Government House, on a platform decorated with flags and a portrait of Her Majesty the Queen.[5] And on June 26, 1843, Imperial Chinese Commissioner Keying entered the new reception-room for ceremonial exchange of the ratifications of the 1842 Treaty of Nanking under which Hong Kong was ceded to Britain in perpetuity. Now at last the island was proclaimed a British crown colony, with Pottinger as

Sir Henry Pottinger: 'Government House will be in front of the Record Office.

its first official Governor to be supported by legislative and executive councils.

The new colony celebrated with a royal salute. 'In the evening,' reported the *Friend of China,* 'a large dinner-party was given at Government House in honour of the Chinese Commissioner, who with his suite enjoyed themselves merrily.'

The summer of 1843 was not in general a merry one. A severe outbreak of fever killed hundreds including Gordon's assistant, Captain De Havilland, and laid low everyone else in the Land Office. Pottinger's own assistant, Johnston, had to go home on sick leave at the end of it.

To help get public works moving again, the Governor appointed to replace De Havilland 'Mr Cleverly, a professional surveyor who lately came out from England'. And to help ease the shortage of government accommodation, he took over the house that Johnston was vacating, a house he himself had authorised Johnston to build, on the bluff near Murray Battery above the parade ground. Pottinger rented it in the name of the government, writing Johnston an outraged letter about his proviso that the house was to be handed back in the same state of repair as it was found. Considering that this proviso was directed at the Governor of Hong Kong, he fumed, it was 'to say the least of it, in extreme bad taste'. The required monthly rent of $150 per month would be paid (it was a seller's market) but repairs must come out of Johnston's own pocket.[6]

Pottinger was a fighter. Gordon, his Land Officer, had produced a town plan which envisaged church, government offices and law courts all on Government Hill, with the Government House higher up 'as at present, isolated from all other buildings';[7] and Pottinger, who liked the plan, fought hard during 1843 against a rival plan, by Commanding Royal Engineer Major Aldrich, that would encroach on his cherished hill and appropriate much of the town centre for the military.

None the less, at one of the first meetings of the legislative council in January 1844, he announced that he considered Major-General D'Aguilar, newly arrived, to be 'fully entitled to a residence at the public expense', both in his capacity of Commander of Her Majesty's Forces in China and in that of Lieutenant-Governor of Hong Kong. A few weeks later, he endorsed D'Aguilar's decision to start building himself a residence without waiting for permission from London. Since the rent demanded for the only available house suitable for a GOC and his staff was $400 per month, an official residence would constitute 'a great saving'.[8]

At the same time, in a despatch discussing expenditure on 'the whole of the buildings at present included under the name of the Government House', Pottinger asked the Secretary of State for War and the Colonies which civil officers were to be provided with residences. Lord Stanley replied that the Governor was the only one to be given a residence and $70,000 had been budgeted for building it.[9]

Then, $70,000 was approximately £14,500. The budget for Hong Kong's Government House may be compared for interest with the £167,000 that had been spent by Lord Wellesley at the start of the century to build himself the Government House palace in Calcutta, and against the fantastic sums that were still being spent on the trappings of gubernatorial office all over British India, whose Governor-General alone had a bodyguard of 130 men, a stable of 146 elephants . . .

But Pottinger's query about residences was disinterested. He had tendered his resignation shortly after Keying's visit and by the time Stanley's frugal reply arrived he had left Hong Kong for good – already promised, it was said, the plum governorship of Madras.

Gordon's map, December 1843

2

Johnston's house
to Caine's house (1844-48)

Pottinger's successor, John Francis Davis, claimed to be content to leave a permanent Government House until last but rarely missed a chance to point out the lack of one.

He arrived in May 1844, was sworn in 'at the Government-house, Victoria', received an issue of Government House furniture, and from Government House promptly sent a despatch about the accommodation situation to Lord Stanley.

'No residence at present exists for the Governor of this colony,' he wrote, 'beyond a detached ground floor of only three rooms, run up in the course of a few weeks for the reception of Keying in the summer of 1843. Behind this is another detached ground floor of two or three rooms, in which the Private Secretary sleeps. The inconvenience as well as unhealthiness of such an abode might tempt me to incur an outlay of not more than £10,000 on account of a Government House, according to a plan and estimate now preparing; but I feel great reluctance to proceed on this without Your Lordship's approval and until the lapse of this summer shall have determined whether the sickness and mortality of last year proceeded from the season merely or from the public residence having been fixed on the north side of the ridge of which this island consists.'[1]

Davis did not choose to stay in the Keying bungalow. By August, his despatches had ceased to be headed 'Government House' and he was living in Johnston's house on the bluff, the one rented by Pottinger. It was a substantial, two-storey home with capacious rooms and a wide verandah running around three sides – clearly more comfortable than anything up at the Record Office.

'My own present residence (lately the Land Office),' Davis told Stanley in August, 'is quite commodious enough to enable me to dispense with any other one until orders shall be received from home for its erection but the actual condition of the temporary public offices, always frail and unsubstantial, may probably render necessary the commencement of permanent ones at an early period.'[2]

A list of government buildings subsequently supplied by Davis to London shows which ones he was referring to. 'Government Offices Nos 1 and 2' are described respectively as 'the building erected for the reception of Keying by Sir Henry Pottinger' now used as a state room and offices by Governor, council, etc; and as 'the earliest building in the colony' now used as, e.g., Land and Record offices. Both are stated to be 'in very bad condition'. Buildings listed as rented by the government include 'Mr Johnston's house formerly used as a Land Office adjoining parade ground. Present residence of His Excellency the Governor'.[3] Gordon's Land Office may have moved uphill as the Governor moved down.

Four days after telling London he could dispense for the time being with a proper Government House, Davis forwarded a blistering

Johnston's house (extreme left, centre)
adjoining parade ground.

memorandum by R. M. Martin, the new Colonial Treasurer, who said he had sought in vain for one valuable quality in Hong Kong and could see no justification for the British government spending a shilling on the place. Davis, receiving a salary of £6,000 plus accommodation, said Martin was too recent an arrival to know what he was talking about.

In his initial despatch about the unhealthy Keying bungalow, Davis had mentioned a plan for a permanent Government House. To this plan – just submitted to him by Gordon, now called Surveyor General – the Governor never voluntarily referred again. His opinion of Gordon, as of much else that he found in Hong Kong, was low; and by March 1845 he was telling Stanley that, except for the officers of the ordnance department, there was scarcely anyone in the colony capable of producing plans for a public building.

At the beginning of May 1845, Davis sent in the colony's first Blue Book, commenting that 'the principal remaining sources of initiatory and extraordinary expenditure are the church, the Government Offices and court of justice and the Governor's residence – which last I am quite content to postpone until all others are completed'.

The spate of despatches with which he followed up, casts some doubt on the claim to contentment. Even if the four public buildings outstanding had been sanctioned by London, Davis wrote a week later, Hong Kong's Land Office was not up to the job. He would like the ordnance department to take over; in fact, Major Aldrich had already volunteered.

In June, Davis wrote that Aldrich was drawing up plans for public buildings but that Johnston's house might be purchased for use as a court house. And in July he elaborated on this idea.

'I have to propose to Your Lordship as a measure of economy,' he wrote to Stanley, 'that the house at present hired for my own residence, if approved by a board of survey, be purchased of the proprietor to serve as a court house, for which it is well adapted, as soon as a Government House shall have been erected . . . The early purchase of this property will be a measure of economy as it was hired, according to the existing high rates of rental, at $1,800 per annum.'[4]

Far from recommending postponement of an official residence for the Governor of Hong Kong, Davis was now suggesting one be built as soon as possible. A month later, in August 1845, he forwarded Aldrich's plans for both Government Offices and a Government House.

The despatch crossed with one from the Secretary of State asking to see Gordon's plans. The Surveyor General, in England on sick leave and temporarily replaced by Cleverly, had mentioned having designed before his departure both a Government House and a church. Davis immediately forwarded a coloured sketch and rough floor plans for a colonnaded two-storey house plus plans for a church, maintaining that both designs were useless without more detail than Gordon had supplied.

'Not insensible, however, to the importance of suitable public offices (however I might contrive to make shift for a residence),' he wrote piously, 'I urged the Acting Surveyor General, soon after Mr Gordon's departure, to furnish me with working drawings and detailed estimates to transmit home . . . Longer experience and a comparison of the buildings raised by the Land Office and those executed by the ordnance department caused me to apply to Major Aldrich for his assistance.'

Gordon had said that his Government House could be built of the best materials for about £10,500. Aldrich had informed Davis the job could not be done under £15,000. Davis trusted that the ordnance department's plans would now be approved.[5]

By 1846, the Governor was less sanguine. Pushed by the home government, he had started to raise a local revenue and was being reviled for it both by the merchants and by a press that was quoting his high salary and complaining about Government House feasts at public expense. He had sent plans for public buildings to London and still received no authority to start work on them.

'I am at length compelled to abandon my present residence, the old Land Office,' he wrote in February, 'on account of its close vicinity to the newly erected barracks, and the constant noise of drums and bugles necessarily attending them. Extensive military works also will soon be commenced immediately adjoining the house. I therefore purpose giving up the present unsuitable premises occupied as a court house at the monthly rent of $180, and using my present residence, the former Land Office, hired at only $150 per month, as a court house for which it is better suited . . .

'As long as a Government House remains unbuilt, I am compelled to provide myself with any residence that the existing state of the colony affords. On quitting my present residence, I have engaged a house lately completed not far from Government Offices, at a monthly rental of $250 from the first instant. This sum may seem high but the Major-General Commanding occupies at present a much inferior residence for which $400 a month has been paid since his arrival.'[6]

At this point in his despatch, Davis received one from Stanley approving the general arrangements he had made for the public buildings, asking for more details from Aldrich but authorising work on the new Government Offices to proceed in any case, to ensure the safety of the public records.

Caine's House, the Governor's new 'palace' up the hill.

The house Davis had now rented was an oddly-shaped place just put up by William Caine, the Magistrate, on the site of today's Roman Catholic Cathedral. The lease, which the Governor signed in person, committed him to maintaining premises, grounds and trees in good order, and Caine to keeping the house 'sound and watertight'. At $3,000 or £625 a year, the rent was nearly double that of Johnston's house.[7]

The *Friend of China*, when it found out, sailed into the attack.

'Magnificent quarters for the military officers and their Chief are nearly completed. The Governor, if he has not built himself a palace, pays the rent of one for his own accommodation out of the public purse.' How was it then, the paper thundered, that the established church had only a matshed for its services?[8]

That autumn, tenders were finally invited for the construction of proper Government Offices *and* church. Major-General D'Aguilar moved into the handsome Head Quarter House (today's Flagstaff House) that he had built himself above the harbour.[9] But there was no move on a Government House. Davis, away north much of the year and under mounting fire back in Hong Kong, had dropped the subject and so apparently had the home government.

In March 1847, Davis forwarded the Blue Book for the previous year with the comment that building works in progress comprised nearly everything required bar a court house and Government House 'which I have left to the last'.

The following month Aldrich returned to England and Davis led an expedition against Canton. In August, he resigned. The resignation did not take practical effect until 1848 but there were no more exchanges about a Government House. The Governor signed off with a request merely for permission to level the site selected on Government Hill.

At the same time, he proposed that public works be handled in future by the Surveyor General. Gordon had resigned at the end of 1846 and the post was now held by Charles St George Cleverly.

The Caine-Davis lease, signed in February 1846.

3

Caine's house
to Spring Gardens (1848-50)

Hong Kong's third Governor, Samuel George Bonham, was a very different character from both Pottinger and Davis. A sociable man, he liked his comforts and made it plain from the start that he wanted a proper residence. He had been Governor of the Straits Settlements for the last 10 years; he was used to having not one but a string of Government Houses at his disposal.

Even before he left for Hong Kong, the Colonial Office had been alerted to the fact that he would be taking his family out. A Government House, it predicted, would be of more importance to him than to Davis who had left his family at home.

Bonham took office in March 1848. Within a week he had set up a committee to report on the state of the Caine residence he had inherited from Davis. The committee (headed by Caine who was now Colonial Secretary) came straight back saying the house needed painting upstairs and down, its wicket gate needed attention, its sedan chairs should be replaced and some 70 new items of furniture were required including mahogany chairs, fireplace screens and a punkah.

Bonham started prodding the home government. 'My Lord,' he wrote in April to Earl Grey who was by now the Secretary of State, 'The house which I am allowed by government is by no means a bad one, and perhaps under all circumstances the best adapted for the purpose that can be procured, the site on which it stands being agreeable, and the public rooms in some degree suitable; but it contains only two bedrooms with dressing-rooms. This private accommodation was perhaps sufficient for my predecessor who had not his family with him, but as my family is with me, I have no spare room for the accommodation of my staff; and as it is essential that they should have their residence in the vicinity of the Government House, I have hired a small house for their accommodation at Spanish $60 per month, or £150 per annum, which in this colony is as low as a decent and fitting accommodation can be procured for.

'Under this explanation I trust Your Lordship will be pleased to sanction this small expense, which of course will cease on the completion of a Government House, which is now nearly the only building to be erected.'[1]

In May, Bonham followed through and brought Cleverly forward.

'My Lord,' he wrote again, 'My predecessor in his Despatch No. 40 of 13th March last, proposed to Your Lordship that in future all civil works should be executed by the Surveyor General, and I now have the honor to enclose a plan and approximate estimate for a Government House which have been prepared in that department by Mr Cleverly, the Surveyor General. The plan appears to me well calculated for the purpose, and offering conveniences and comforts both suitable and essential. The more complete estimate enumerating

Governor Bonham: despatch after despatch.

Victoria, Hongkong,
22nd May, 1848.

My Lord,

My Predecessor in his Despatch No. 40
the 15th March last proposed to your Lordship
t in future all Civil Works should be
ucted by the Surveyor General, and I now
the honor to enclose a Plan and approximate
imate for a Government House which have
prepared in that Department by Mr
ly, the Surveyor General. The Plan appears
e well calculated for the purpose, and
ing conveniences and comforts both suitable
d essential. The more complete estimate
merating the necessary details and
ring into all particulars connected with
service, will be forwarded by the next mail

Right Honorable

Major Aldrich, I am in hopes that objection
will not be taken to the proposed mansion
on the ground of expense.

I have the honor to be,
With the highest respect,
Your Lordship's,
Most Obedient
Humble Servant,

the necessary details, and entering into all particulars connected with this service, will be forwarded by the next mail.

'With regard to locality and public convenience, there is no building in this colony adapted for a Government House; and though the one I now occupy may be justly considered as a desirable residence, and indeed as to position better than any other at present procurable; still its want of room renders it desirable that a Government House should be commenced upon with as little delay as possible.'

Davis, Bonham told Grey, had in August 1845 sent home a plan by Major Aldrich for a house that would cost £14,407. Since this new Cleverly plan was better suited to Hong Kong's climate and no more costly, he hoped objection would not be made to it because of expense.[2]

Cleverly was equally verbose, equally at pains to assure that there was nothing extravagant about his plan.

'In accordance with His Excellency's instructions,' he wrote, 'I have prepared the design with the strictest care as to economy, at the same time with sufficient regard to its character and stability and necessary requirements for a residence in this variable climate.

'The house, servants' offices, stables, gate lodge and guard house, gates to offices, laying out and enclosing the ground I propose shall not exceed the original approximate estimate prepared by Major Aldrich for the house and offices alone . . .'[3]

Cleverly's rough estimate.

Spring Gardens and (right) the Blenkin Rawson house.

The following month, June 1848, tenders were publicly invited for levelling a site. A contractor called Assen got the job, to be completed by the end of the year.[4]

At the end of July, Bonham forwarded to England Cleverly's detailed estimate for a house costing £14,940; and in September he wrote to Grey again. On his arrival in Hong Kong, the Governor disclosed, he had found such an inferior collection of furniture in use at Government House that, on the recommendation of a committee he had set up to look into the matter, he had spent £284 on furnishing the public rooms in a more becoming manner.

'This furniture is respectable in its kind, without being unnecessarily expensive,' he assured, 'and will hereafter form a part of that which will be required for the public apartments of the Government House which I presume at no distant period will be constructed.'[5]

At this juncture, Caine's house having changed hands, Bonham moved himself, family and new furniture a mile out of town to a house at Spring Gardens belonging to a firm by the name of Blenkin, Rawson. The house, which today would be in the heart of Wan Chai, stood in half an acre of land fronted by ornamental gardens giving straight onto the waterfront. Hong Kong's Overseer of Roads, M. Bruce, had done a pleasant drawing of it in 1846 and botanist Robert Fortune now commended its grounds. Some of the houses, he wrote in reference to the Hong Kong of 1848, 'have really beautiful gardens. I may instance those of His Excellency at "Spring Gardens", of Messrs Dent and Co. at "Green Bank" and of Messrs Jardine and Matheson at "East Point".'[6]

Bonham's optimistic despatch about a permanent Government House had crossed, however, with one from Grey suddenly ordering him to slash total expenditure 'at whatever inconvenience and sacrifice'. Revised estimates had shown up a probable deficit and that deficit, said Grey, was not going to be made up from a bigger parliamentary grant. In fact, the annual grant to Hong Kong was going to be progressively diminished. The colony must learn to rely on its own resources.

Bonham reeled, stopped all possible public works and even delayed drawing his own salary to help balance the new budget. Fortunately, the rent of his new Spring Gardens residence was exactly the same as the rent of Caine's house, and the extra house for the servants could be dispensed with.

Grey had not, however, specifically forbidden Bonham to build a Government House. General approval was given of Cleverly's plans (provided, cautioned the Treasury, these did not appear to Earl Grey 'to comprise any such superfluity of accommodation or ornament as should call for particular remark or revision') and left it to the Governor to decide when the time was right.

For and against

A PERIOD of strict retrenchment followed, during which the *Friend of China* aired its own ideas on economising – ideas that included scrapping some of the most important posts in the colony.

'The offices of a military Commandant and Governor ought to be held by one person,' announced the paper in June 1849. 'Such a combination has this recommendation, £500 a year will be saved to the revenue – that rent being paid for the house now occupied by Mr Bonham.' And why were the posts of Surveyor General and Colonial Engineer retained, 'pressing the heart's blood out of a colony still struggling for its existence', when their jobs could be done for a few hundred pounds a year by the Royal Engineers? 'Is it,' asked the unfriendly *Friend*, 'that there may be a few idle danglers about Government House; men who wear unexceptionable ties and drive about in straw-coloured kid gloves?'[7]

In August, the paper attacked again. 'Retrenchment should begin at Government House,' it declared. The offices of Surveyor General and Colonial Engineer were superfluous encumbrances. What public works were in hand, after all? A court house had finally been purchased, the Government Offices were finished, the colonial church was in use. 'We hope there is no intention of squandering the money' (Hong Kong's budget) 'upon an expensive Government House. The house built for the military Commander-in-Chief is well suited for the Governor's residence.'[8]

This time Bonham reacted, with two despatches to London. One enclosed the Estimates for 1850, allowing £6,000 towards a new Government House. The other justified construction of that house on grounds of both economy and dignity of office.

Some grates and mantelpieces sent out from England provided the immediate excuse. The fittings, Bonham wrote, had been ordered for the new Government House and, since he could not establish whether they had been paid for, he must make some allowance for settlement of the £1,815 bill. As His Lordship would have seen, he had taken every opportunity to reduce colony expenditure with the result that, even taking this furniture bill into account, he expected a surplus of some £4,500 at the end of 1849. This, he would like to devote to the commencement of a Government House – if Lord Grey could just assure him of continuing parliamentary grants for 1850 and 1851 so that he could allocate £6,000 and £2,625 for those years also, thus realising the full £14,940 of Cleverly's estimate.[9]

Grey smiled on Bonham and his sums. 'I think a house absolutely necessary,' he scribbled across the despatch when he read it. 'I am not able to judge what it ought to cost but it would be very bad economy not to build a good one.'

In March 1850, assured by Bonham that the colony's financial embarrassments were over, Grey made it official. 'I am satisfied,' he wrote, 'that the time has come when the erection of a proposed Government House may with propriety be commenced.'

Simultaneously, as it happened, one of the colony's big trading companies wrote to Bonham with a novel proposal: that the government buy Green Bank as a Government House. Green Bank was the house whose gardens Fortune had praised along with those at Spring Gardens and East Point. It stood, Dent and Company now claimed, in the most central part of town, in three acres of exotic garden planted with flowers and trees from all over the world. With the addition of a carriage entrance onto Wyndham Street and a third storey for which Surveyor General Cleverly had already drawn up plans, it would make an excellent residence for the Governor. Some $50,000 had been spent on it; it was offered to the government for $25,000 including a costly new iron verandah . . .

Dent's dangled the carrot of comfort in front of the Governor, still living in rented accommodation at Spring Gardens. Start the suggested alterations at the end of the approaching rainy season, they said, 'and a complete and handsome Government House will be in readiness within a year from the present time.'

Since the mail from London still took two to three months, Dent's proposal reached Bonham long before Grey's sanction to build. He dismissed it out of hand none the less. 'The house in question, considering its locality and other circumstances connected with it,' he told Grey, 'is totally unsuited for the purpose.'[10]

4 The house Cleverly built
(1851-58)

BONHAM stayed at Spring Gardens until the end of his governor-ship, living several years in the Blenkin Rawson property and then moving next door to a three-storey house belonging to Turner and Company – a house with a 'fine well of spring water' in its larger grounds and abutting today's Spring Garden Lane. His rent stayed the same at £625 a year: it was a buyer's market now and Spring Gardens was no longer the desirable residence it had been.[1]

Construction on the new Government House did not start in earn-est until October 1851, although the ground for it had been levelled three years previously and the old Record Office opposite handed over to Cleverly as a works site. By this time all the money was to hand but Bonham (like Davis before him) had resignation in mind and had lost his initial enthusiasm for the project, even to the extent of suggesting what the *Friend of China* had suggested earlier: that the Governor should take the GOC's house as his residence.

Cleverly's plans for a Government House, which owed something to those of both Gordon and Aldrich and which he credited George Strachan in his office with drawing up, called for a neo-classical mansion, pillared on all four sides.

The gate-lodge and main entrance faced south to Victoria Peak. At ground level, an open verandah led past offices through to a pil-lared hall the height of the house. Off that hall, on the left, were stairs then dining-room; on the right, library then drawing-room. Hall, dining-room and drawing-room all gave onto a second open verandah facing the harbour. From this an important, balustraded flight of steps led down to the grounds. Upstairs were half a dozen bedrooms, nursery, another drawing-room and more verandahs.

The whole house was to be 117 by 96 feet and, because of the slope of the land, two-thirds of it would have a basement, connecting by covered ways to outlying kitchen and stable blocks.[2]

By February 1852, Cleverly was able to report some site prepara-tion and the employment of over 2,000 convicts on road works that eventually produced Upper Albert Road. The following month, a contract was let for construction of the house itself.

Bonham at this stage went home on sick leave. From Head Quarter House, Major-General Jervois stood in for him as Acting Governor while Dr John Bowring, Britain's Consul at Canton, took over as Plenipotentiary and Superintendent of Trade. It was a source of annoyance to some residents that Hong Kong should have to pay the entire £6,000 salary of its man at the top when at least half his work was on behalf of British residents in China; and Bowring aggravated the feeling by moving into Bonham's residence.

'His Excellency Dr Bowring has, by instructions from home,' grumbled the *China Mail* of April 29, 1852, 'taken possession of Government House – to which we see only two objections: the one,

Cleverly's plans: the main entrance of his Government House facing Victoria Harbour.

that the Foreign Office has no *right* to quarter its officials upon the colony; the other, that the house is too far distant from the centre of town for forenoon calls. This latter objection, however, is obviated by Dr Bowring's being always to be found from 11 to past four at the Superintendency offices.'

The *Friend of China* was always delighted to be able to disagree with the *Mail* and on May 5 it ran a sarcastic letter to the editor. Whatever did Dr Bowring find to *do* at his office to stay there such long hours, asked the writer, 'and which is the particular part of town known as the centre from whence Spring Garden Palace is so inconveniently far distant?'

Jervois and Bowring stayed in joint control for nearly a year. When Bonham finally returned in February 1853 there was a lot to say about progress, or lack of it, on Upper Albert Road and Cleverly promptly said it.

'The government having decided upon the erection of Government House from designs prepared by me for that work, and adequate assistance not existing in the department for its effective supervision,' he reported, 'the services of three sappers (a carpenter, bricklayer and stone-mason) were placed at my disposal.

Cleverly's plans: the general site, opposite the old Record Office.

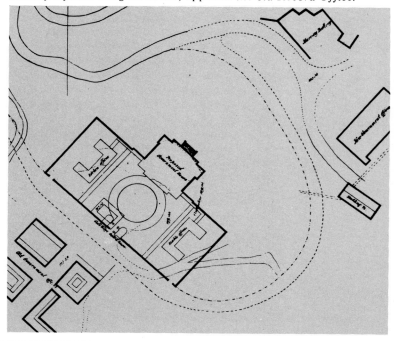

Cleverly's plans: the ground floor.

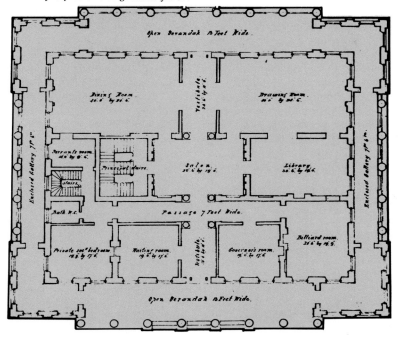

'The work has apparently proceeded rather slowly, but this is naturally the case where a large quantity of material has to be cut and prepared before it can be built in . . .

'Suffice it to say that my best energies shall be exerted to render the whole building as perfect a specimen of work as the means at my disposal will enable me to effect, and trust that in 10 months from the present date the building and offices with it will be finished, so that it may be fit for occupation in the beginning of April 1854.'

Cleverly, by now a prominent local figure and Freemason – the man from County Cork who had built the Cathedral and Zetland Lodge and been presented with a cup for his improvements to the race-course at Happy Valley – felt all the importance of this particular commission.

He revealed some of his building techniques with pride. The basement of the new house, he said, was entirely arched over in brick and thus made fire-proof, 'besides preventing the ascent of noise and effluvia from the cellars'. A thorough system of ventilation had been adopted, with the fresh air being admitted and discharged only from the verandahs; and for maximum stability, the marble floors of the verandahs were also supported upon arches, with the spandrels formed hollow to lighten the weight.

As little timber as possible was being introduced and where its use was unavoidable, he had taken every available measure against white ants, dry rot, etc: 'that is, in addition to the extensive system of ventilation alluded to, I have thoroughly coated it with coal tar wherever it is inserted in the walls; and previously to the laying down the floors I intend to wash the whole with a solution of arsenic, as well as adding another coat of tar where practicable. With these precautions I hope much of the damage so common to almost all the buildings in the colony will be avoided.'[3]

Bonham could not stay to listen or to watch. The Taiping rebels were threatening British interests in Shanghai and, a month after his return from leave, he had to sail north.

Bowring's choice

In September 1853, the Governor found time to send home Cleverly's estimate of £1,031 for furnishing the new house.[4] It met with rare approval. 'Very moderate for a Government House in an oriental colony,' was the immediate reaction. 'It would be difficult to furnish a house of very limited size in London for less than that.'

It was 1854, however, before an official reply was sent and then it was addressed not to Bonham but to Bowring who had been appointed to succeed him. Acceptance of Cleverly's furniture estimate, wrote the Duke of Newcastle as Secretary of State, depended partly on whether Bowring decided to live in the new house.

A major shake-up was pending. On Bonham's departure, the home government planned to separate control of the colony from control of British affairs in China. Caine was to be Lieutenant-Governor in charge of the island. Bowring was to be styled Plenipotentiary, Superintendent of Trade and Governor of Hong Kong like his predecessors – but he was to be Governor in name only and receive a salary of £4,000 instead of £6,000.

Bowring, back in England, already over 60 years of age, had accepted the commission and then penned Newcastle a spirited plea for more money, based on his recent experience of the cost·of living at Spring Gardens.

'It is intended no doubt,' he wrote in December 1853 from the Athenaeum, 'that I should occupy the new Government House – built on a large and expensive scale harmonising with the large salary appropriated by Parliament to the united offices of Governor and Plenipotentiary. Your Grace proposes, as is indeed most desirable, that the Plenipotentiary should be relieved from a large portion of the cares and duties connected with the colony, but he cannot be relieved from heavy expenses which fall upon him in his quality of Governor and as occupier of the Government House.

'In Hong Kong, where there are no commodious hotels and very few commercial establishments in a condition to receive guests, the claims upon the hospitality of the Governor are frequently irresistible. Not only are many English gentlemen officially recommended to him from all parts of the world but distinguished foreigners, many occupying elevated official positions, naturally expect those attentions with which high functionaries are in the habit of welcoming one another. The fleets of many great nations are now in the China Seas, frequently making Hong Kong their headquarters – while the peopling of Western America, as well as the tides of emigration to Australia, are immensely extending the field and the activity of our intercourse both public and private in China; and I may be allowed to add that Hong Kong is one of the dearest places in the world.'[5]

Bowring's eloquence did him little good. The new house was merely offered to him, he was informed; its use was not compulsory. Newcastle followed up with the proviso about money for furniture.

On his return to Hong Kong in April 1854 to take up office, Bowring 'landed at Government House' – apparently still the Turner property at Spring Gardens, with a rent pegged at £625 a year – and gave a ball there the following month for the Queen's birthday. He expressed no interest in the Government House under construction but neither did he express any intention of not using it when it was finished.

Lieutenant-Governor Caine, on a salary of only £2,000 without any official residence, submitted a plea to London for a modest housing allowance – and got it.

Progress on site

CLEVERLY meanwhile toiled on at Upper Albert Road. He had hoped to have the house fit for occupation by April 1854 and go off to England on leave, but it would not be ready, it seemed, until the end of the year.

'New Government House progressed very slowly indeed,' he reported for 1853's Blue Book, 'in consequence of the partial failure of the contractor and a strike amongst the masons, to whom a considerable amount of money being due, I was obliged to make arrangements myself for payment.'

The three sappers were doing a good job but since their assistance was confined to Government House, he had had to supervise all other public works himself alone and these had comprised debtors' prison, treadwheel house, gaoler's residence, police-station, two school-houses . . .[6] The list was long and a difficult year passed.

March 1855 and Cleverly was even more harassed. Government House was still not finished, despite his efforts.

'The contractor and his securities received notice that the bonds would be enforced if more active progress was not made,' he stated, 'but they complained that it was impossible to obtain some materials unless at a most exorbitant rate, and others could not be obtained at all in consequence of the troubles in Canton and the numerous hoardes of pirates which infest the approaches, laying embargoes upon all Chinese vessels passing to and fro . . .

'For instance, during the greater part of the year but little lime has reached the colony from the neighbourhood of Canton, and the supply has been made almost entirely from the kilns on the opposite Kowloon shore, for which an exorbitant price was demanded.

'Fortunately, before the blockade I obtained nearly all the marble tiles I required; the deficiency, however, I have supplied by slate and stone. The earthenware railings for the verandah I am still unable to get from Fushan where such articles are made; and I have totally failed in procuring gypsum for the fine mouldings and enrichments of the cornices and ceilings; thus I have been obliged to alter the designs in a material degree, which I much regret. However the work, slowly as it has progressed, is admirably executed, and is perhaps as perfect a building as can be erected in China.

'Unfortunately, at a time when I required the most efficient super-intendence, the sappers attached to the department were ordered home, and at the end of August I was deprived of their services altogether. The want of these men I have felt greatly, particularly in all plumber's and bell-hanger's work (at which the Chinese are very deficient), so that my personal superintendence upon each particular piece of work during execution was rendered absolutely necessary.'

The Surveyor General further bewailed delays on all the out-buildings; difficulties with the water supply; the death of trees planted in the grounds; the tiresome 80-foot drop to the west of the house; and his own deteriorating health caused partly, he said, by his never in nearly 12 years having had any leave of absence to England.[7]

His troubles in this context were nearly over. By October 1, 1855 – four years precisely since the start of construction, more than 12 years since Hong Kong was declared a colony and Cleverly was signed on – Government House proper was ready for occupation.

'The whole service as executed,' sighed Cleverly with relief before departing at last on home leave, 'has given much satisfaction to my-self and I have no doubt to His Excellency, but although it cannot be compared with a first rate English-built house, it is substantial and exceedingly handsome.

'The services, though hardly finally completed, have been executed considerably within the estimate, and do credit to Chinese work. The arching of the verandahs is admirable.'

First tenants

EMBARRASSINGLY, the Governor's rented accommodation had been sold before the Upper Albert Road house was finished, necessitating special arrangements with the new proprietors to allow him to stay on.

Despite this, Bowring was not eager for the move. The scheme under which Caine was in administrative control of Hong Kong had been terminated in mid-1855 as unworkable and Bowring was full Governor – but still on £4,000 a year. He had told Newcastle before he came out that life in the new Government House would be expensive and now he laboured his point, trying for a rise.

'The cost of living in the colony is enormous,' he protested in September 1855. 'In my quality as Governor, heavy expenses fall upon me and whether I am present or absent from the island the fixed charges of the establishment are very heavy. These are now about to be considerably augmented by my early removal to a large house built on a scale appropriate to governors always hitherto paid at the rate of £6,000 a year.'[8]

There were other problems. The contractor who had given Cleverly such trouble eventually failed and one of his guarantors had to be taken to prison before he would pay up, while some of the subcontractors had to be fined.

Then the main contractor died, obliging Bowring to make a gratuity to his widow who was left destitute.[9]

Worse, within days of the Bowrings moving in, a second death occurred on the premises.

'Some Chinese were engaged yesterday afternoon in getting a flagstaff erected in front of the new Government house,' reported the *Friend of China* on October 3, 'when the shears, mast and all went down with a run, killing one man outright and severely damaging two others. The shears and mast falling into the verandah, must have created considerable alarm in the family of His Excellency the Governor, who have only moved in to the building within the last few days . . . What can Chinese,' the paper asked callously, 'even though they be ship carpenters, know about rigging derricks?'

Some of the furniture for the house had still not arrived from England. The roof caused problems. So did the water supply, initially left in the hands of the military. 'His Excellency the Governor,' said Cleverly's stand-in, discussing the first year of residence on Upper Albert Road, 'is well aware how miserably this supply has failed . . . Indeed it was never turned on till 3.30 pm and never reached Government House until 8 pm and more frequently towards the latter end of the year never reached it at all.'[10]

Still, the first Christmas in the new house was celebrated comfortably enough, with a Christmas Day party that included – besides Bowring, his wife and two daughters – Rear-Admiral Sir James Stirling, and George Henry Preble currently serving under Commodore Perry on the American expedition that opened up Japan.

'We had a very social dinner and a pleasant evening,' noted Preble in his diary. 'The dinner table was brilliant with plates, glass and wax lights. The only toasts were Victoria, Napoleon III and Gen. Pearce, proposed by Sir John Bowring. Lady B's plum pudding was praised as a matter of course by all the guests and discussion as to the orthodox method of cutting it was had, the Admiral siding for slices instead of wedges as that left the remainder right for the fry next day.

'Lady Bowring is so lame,' Preble added, 'it is painful to see her go from room to room on her crutches. She told me the other day that she was 62 years old.'[11]

On New Year's Day, the Bowrings gave a ball and soon Bowring was trying again for more money, grumbling to the Secretary of State that the 'beautiful and palatial edifice' he had been given to live in was hard to keep up on a salary of £4,000.

Government House, a painting in 1858 from above Murray Barracks.

'I may be permitted to say,' he repeated, 'that as Governor many expenses are necessarily imposed upon me; that the cost of living is enormously augmented in the colony in consequence of its prosperity; that the Government House (first occupied by me) was built for a functionary whose salary was understood to be £6,000 a year; that only the official apartments of that large building are furnished at the public expense while my predecessor (and myself during the first 18 months of my residence in the colony) occupied a completely furnished house at a cost to the colony of £600 a year.'[12]

The protest fell on deaf ears but Bowring's attention was in any case distracted from domestic expenses by a public dispute that broke out between his Chief Justice and Attorney General – a dispute stemming from Attorney General Anstey's contention that Justice Hulme had been drunk at an official Government House dinner, receiving the toast to the Queen in an 'uproarious and silly way'[13] – and by the *Arrow* war that he himself precipitated with China. The hostilities led, among other things, to the attempted poisoning with arsenic bread of Hong Kong's foreign residents, including the Governor's family; and Bowring's initiative found small favour in Britain. He lost his cherished title of Plenipotentiary to Lord Elgin, whom he had to host at the new Government House in 1857 and who concluded the June 1858 Treaty of Tientsin that permitted Britain to establish diplomatic relations with Peking.

Bowring's authority, which he had been proud to say embraced Japan, Siam, China and Korea, was now in effect limited to Hong Kong island; and it was there, one day in August 1858, that Victorian entertainer Albert Smith found him, quietly picking flowers in the Government House grounds.

'To breakfast at Sir John Bowring's,' starts the entry in Smith's diary, 'walking up pretty winding paths, with the wild convolvulus and bamboo blooming all the way. Found him in the garden . . .'

The entertainer was invited up to the house several times during his month's stay at the Hong Kong Club, on Queen's Road.

Once, after dinner, the party was joined by the Bishop of Victoria and his wife, with some other English residents. 'We had some music,' wrote Smith, 'and I was astonished to find how fresh some of my old songs came out. It was a very agreeable evening.'

Another time, when a Jardine was among the guests, 'Good conversation never ceased, and we had great fun about some wine that Sir John had received from Japan, than which nothing could be nastier. There is a report, tonight, from Sir Robert Maclure, that the Chinese are shuffling about the treaty. At night, coming home, all the chairs and their lanterns, following one another down the winding path to the town, had a pretty effect.'[14]

5

Path to the Peak
(1859-68)

THE following spring Bowring, now in his late sixties, was allowed to resign. He left on May 5 and the following day Lane, Crawford announced a public auction at Government House of his furniture. Terms of sale: cash in Mexican dollars.

Sir Hercules Robinson who took over from Bowring was half his age, had only part of his already-reduced title ('Superintendent of Trade' having gone to the new British Minister to Peking), and a salary cut now to £3,000.

Hong Kong's youngest Governor arrived in September 1859 to find the private apartments of Government House 'nothing but bare walls, with the exception of a few chairs and tables which from time to time had been drafted upstairs as they became unfit for the rooms below. There was no hotel to which I could well have gone; furniture cannot here be purchased ready made. There was no option but to borrow from our neighbours; and notwithstanding the kindness and liberality with which the immediate wants of my family were supplied, we were subjected to inconvenience and discomfort for many weeks.'

Robinson presented the problem to the legislative council which, to prevent a repetition of what Cleverly described as 'the unseemly spectacle of a public auction' at Government House, voted that the heavy furniture for all rooms should in future be supplied by the colony.

Newcastle, back as Secretary of State, refused to sanction the decision although he gave Robinson £250 to help him out.

The new Governor tried a different approach. An inquiry would show, he wrote home, that in colonies free of financial embarrassment, Government House apartments were normally furnished out of the local revenue. In St Christopher, Antigua and Newfoundland he knew for certain that this was the case; and as for Ceylon, the private apartments of both Queen's House in Colombo and the Pavilion in Kandy were furnished at the public expense, the Governor being charged 10 per cent per annum on the outlay.

In Hong Kong too, Robinson claimed (not altogether correctly), 'from the establishment of the colony until 1855, a Government House thoroughly furnished was provided for Sir Henry Pottinger, Sir John Davis, Sir George Bonham and Sir John Bowring, at an expense to the colony of £600 a year.' There had been no change in the arrangement, he informed Newcastle, until October 1855 at which time, the colony being still dependent on parliamentary grants, Sir John Bowring had furnished the private apartments of the new Government House at his own expense. Upon his departure, as Newcastle was aware, Sir John's furniture had been publicly auctioned.

The whole house, Robinson contended, should now and hence-

Under the hammer: Sir John Bowring's furniture

PUBLIC AUCTION.

LANE, CRAWFORD & Co. beg to intimate that they have received instructions to sell by PUBLIC AUCTION, at *Government House,* on

FRIDAY,

the 13th day of May, 1859,

commencing at Noon, the following belonging to H. E. SIR JOHN BOWRING,—

A quantity of strong and useful FURNITURE, specially adapted for Bed-room use, consisting of Marble-topped and *Ningpo* TABLES BOOKCASES, TEA POYS, WARDROBES, EASY CHAIRS, BEDSTEADS, COUCHES, &c., &c., &c.

Also,

A ROSEWOOD COTTAGE PIANOFORTE, and CANTERBURY.

And,

A complete Set of Massive Elegantly-finished SILVER-PLATE, of English manufacture, comprising — Solid Silver TABLE and DESSERT SPOONS, FORKS, SOUP and SAUCE LADLES, TEA POT, COFFEE POT, MUFFINEERS, &c., &c.; and Electro-plated DISH-COVERS, SALVERS, CURRY DISHES, HOT-WATER DISHES, Drawing Room and Bed Room CANDLESTICKS, WINE COOLERS, &c., &c., &c.

CATALOGUES of the whole will be ready for delivery in a few days.

TERMS OF SALE.—*Cash in* MEXICAN *Dollars, weighed at* 7.1.7.

Queen's Road, 6th May, 1859.

forth be furnished at public expense, perhaps with the Governor paying a percentage as in Ceylon.[1]

Still Newcastle refused, although a decade later the system was adopted.

On the matter of salary, Robinson did better. A bare £3,000, he asserted in January 1860, was insufficient to enable the Governor to do his job properly.

'I may mention,' he stressed like Bowring before him, 'that the expense of living is I believe greater in Hong Kong than in any other part of the world; that the wealth and hospitality of the mercantile community are matters of public notoriety; that the island is the headquarters not only of the military forces stationed in China but the headquarters of the largest naval station out of England, the constant resort of foreign vessels of war; and that it is further constantly visited by strangers and foreign officials of distinction, being the central station of six different lines of steam communication.

'All these circumstances combine to make Hong Kong a most expensive government, and one in which with the present reduced official income it would be impossible for the Governor to maintain that system of hospitable intercourse with those around him which serves to subdue asperities and promote a spirit of social goodwill.'

In Robinson's day: Government House and (centre) Johnston's house

Robinson compared his position with that of, for instance, Hong Kong's Major-General who was getting £4,500 plus a house; and with that of the Governor of Singapore (where the cost of living was 'far less'), who was getting over £4,200. 'I have omitted, I observe, to mention that a residence is provided here for the Governor but, as this was planned when the salary was £6,000 and the expenses of living not two-thirds of what they are at present, it tends rather to add to the embarrassments of the position.'[2]

Newcastle accepted his arguments and raised the Governor's salary to £5,000. By the time the rise came through, Robinson had additional domestic expense in the form of a daughter born at Government House in August 1860.[3]

Two-way expansion

BY now, Britain was again at war with China since the Chinese had refused to ratify Elgin's Treaty of Tientsin. In March 1860, General Sir Hope Grant had arrived in Hong Kong to command a British expedition against China, commenting in passing that he was 'most hospitably received by the Governor, Sir Hercules Robinson, whose residence was beautifully furnished in the English fashion' (the furniture problem had obviously been overcome) 'and well warmed with blazing coal fires.'[4]

In October the treaty was finally ratified and, under a supplementary convention, Kowloon peninsula was – like Hong Kong island before it – ceded in perpetuity to Britain. Robinson became both the first Governor whose brief was confined to the colony and the first whose colony territory had expanded.

In a sense, that territory had begun to expand vertically, too.

Back in 1849, the Colonial Surgeon had recommended building a sanatorium on Victoria Peak to help combat the fever, dysentery and rheumatism bedevilling the settlement. Heat and humidity were the cause of all three ills, Dr William Morrison had declared, and both heat and humidity were markedly less up the mountain.

'The contemplated site of the proposed "sanitarium" is 1,774 feet above the level of the sea,' he had said, 'and by repeated experiment the average range of the thermometer is found to be 10° less at this elevation than it is in the town of Victoria. Moreover the position, which is attainable by a practicable road, is exposed to the s.w. monsoon.' Penang, Singapore and Madeira each already had such a sanatorium. If Hong Kong followed suit, it would obviate all the risks and expense being incurred by those compelled to resort to Macau and elsewhere to regain their health.[5]

Morrison's suggestion was not adopted at the time but 10 years later the War Office had applied for a piece of ground on Victoria

Peak, about 1,700 feet above sea level, to use as an experimental hill sanatorium for the troops. Robinson had assigned the land and cut a path to it at the end of 1859.

From that path developed a hill-station and, ultimately, the whole residential Peak district. But first, almost before the home government realised what was happening, came a mountain home for the Governor.

The sanatorium idea did not work, as far as the War Office was concerned. It opened its little hill hospital, on a plateau just below the summit, in spring 1862. The health of the men sent up there to recuperate, became worse. Army medical officers pronounced the place unhealthy and it was abandoned.

Robinson's successor MacDonnell stepped in, recognising the possibilities of the site. At the beginning of 1867, he bought the sanatorium from the military for a few thousand dollars, resumed the land and wrote to the Secretary of State informing him of his astute move.[6]

That summer, $1,000 was spent on converting the sanatorium's single barrack-room into three separate rooms 'for the use of His Excellency the Governor and officers of the government'. MacDonnell himself made full use of 'Mountain Lodge' until it was destroyed in a typhoon at the end of the season.

The Peak, from newly-ceded Kowloon peninsula

The following spring, the Governor asked his executive council to approve an expenditure of $9,000 on the lodge's reconstruction. He disagreed, he said, with the military's conclusions about the Peak. From March to May it was certainly unpleasant, but as soon as the real heat began it was free of damp. In the summer of 1867, he had lived up there in the old barrack-room for nearly two months. Those who had stayed with him all found the air exhilarating.

Cleverly had finally retired in 1865 and a new Surveyor General now presented plans for a three-room bungalow 'so strong that no future typhoon could seriously damage it for many years', to go up on the same site.

Council raised no objections and MacDonnell sent home an explanatory despatch. He had felt most reluctant, he confessed, to accept the results reported by the medical officers or to regard as concluded the search for a healthier summer climate in the immediate vicinity of the town. He and his friends had used the old sanatorium the previous summer with marked benefit to their health. In such a confined environment as Hong Kong's, the matter was of great public interest. Between town and mountain, there was a temperature difference of up to 14°F – more of a change than could be obtained even from a trip to Japan. He had authorised work to commence on the new lodge. Once it was complete and police had been stationed in the area to allay the general nervousness about hill robbers, he expected many other villas to go up on the Peak.

The Duke of Buckingham, as Secretary of State, asked Mac-Donnell how exactly he intended to apportion use of the new lodge between himself and 'officers of the government'.

'No system other than the simple one of the Governor's occupying it or granting its use has been intended,' admitted MacDonnell. 'I shall probably have to furnish the place and in practice shall either if I am myself there invite those needing a change to occupy any spare accommodation, or lend either the whole or any part of the house and out-buildings in my absence. Even a week's residence there has been known to have a singularly beneficial effect.'[7]

The Colonial Office took his explanation with a pinch of salt.

'Sir Richard MacDonnell calls it a sanatorium,' was one comment, 'but it turns out that he means it to be a Governor's country house.'

'The explanation is just what I expected', said Buckingham, 'but if the change to mountain air is likely to conduce to the health of the Governor . . .' He let it pass.

Two years earlier, when MacDonnell first became Governor, he had sent back a domestic request that had been refused out of hand. Gas lighting had just been introduced to Government House. MacDonnell didn't like it, he didn't want it, and he didn't see why he should pay the bills.

'It was decided before my arrival,' he had complained in a heated, eight-page despatch, 'that Government House should be lit with gas and I found the contractors busy with the preparations for laying the various pipes – causing a general noise, confusion and accumulation of dirt throughout the house so great that even the anticipated cheapness and increased comfort of gas could scarcely repay one for the great discomfort attending the change.

'As personally I much prefer the use of oil and wax lights to that of gas, I would have preferred being left to manage as my predecessors had done before me – especially as the oil lustres and lamps in the reception rooms of Government House were in excellent taste and most effective.

'A vote however had been passed . . . The result has been a degree of discomfort difficult to realize. The gas burners generate smoke and heat with very little light comparatively speaking and – except in the passages and some other places – the gas is a positive nuisance.'

Far from being cheap, it was also extremely expensive, claimed MacDonnell. His gas bills for the house seemed likely to exceed £400 per annum and since he still had to pay for oil burners to supplement the gas – 'so much so that on a late occasion I saw 14 oil burners in my dining-room, in addition to the eight gas burners intended to light the apartment' – his total lighting bills were going to be at least £500, 'an amount absurdly disproportionate to my income, the whole of which is scarcely adequate to meet the rest of my expenditure.'

The gate-lodge, with new gas-lamps

The main entrance, with new gas-lamps

A fair solution, MacDonnell suggested, would be to use public funds to pay for all gas used in the public rooms. 'Short of an absolute injunction' against it from London, he would pass the gas company's bills to the colony for payment.[8]

London promptly sent him that absolute injunction. The Governor's gas bills would in no circumstances be paid by the colony.

Perhaps it was in view of this earlier tussle over his domestic arrangements that the home government saw fit to humour MacDonnell when it came to Mountain Lodge. Or it could be that, with Simla recently established as the official summer seat of government in India, $9,000 to start a hill-station in hot and humid Hong Kong seemed modest enough.

6

The social round
(1869-82)

GOVERNMENT House, Upper Albert Road, was by this stage the social heart of things for the colony's Europeans. Hong Kong was more trading-post than romantic jewel of Empire and its governors never lived in anything approaching the epic style of their counterparts in Calcutta or Madras or Bombay. Still, invitations to Government House were coveted and a social season had established itself around Queen's Birthday celebrations, horse-racing, cricket, club, band concerts in the new public gardens opposite Government House, and those itinerant VIPs successive governors complained it cost so much to host.

Then in 1869, the year that the Suez Canal opened, the VIP sailed in who was to put the royal seal of approval on this expatriate way of life: Alfred, Duke of Edinburgh, 25-year-old second son of Queen Victoria, the first British royal to take a look at Hong Kong.

The Duke stayed two lively weeks as MacDonnell's guest, driving straight to the new City Hall on his arrival on November 2, and then up to Government House along a route lined with infantry to a guard of honour, state banquet and reception.

'During the ceremony,' lyricised the Rev. William Beach, Colonial Chaplain, about the reception given by Lady MacDonnell, 'the hospitalities for which Government House is so famous were extended to a large number of guests; and the fine reception rooms graced on this occasion by the presence of the royal visitor and by that of the fair and the brave, never appeared to greater advantage. The evening was enlivened by the band of Her Majesty's 75th Regiment, which played a selection of fine music, and by dancing; and Government House and grounds were brilliantly illuminated for the occasion. Several German amateurs also kindly entertained the company with pieces of vocal music known to be favourites with the Prince . . . The proceedings were diversified by the passage round Government House of the Chinese Procession of the Dragon and the Fishes.'

A second Government House reception was held during the Duke's stay, with a Guards band playing pieces composed by him. A farewell reception followed on November 15.

'Probably so large an assembly never gathered in Hong Kong on the eve of the departure of the home mail,' observed the chaplain, whom MacDonnell had commissioned to write a souvenir book for the Queen. 'Government House and grounds were beautifully illuminated for the occasion, and the *coup-d'oeil* on entering the gateway was very striking, a most enchanting effect being produced by the thousands of Chinese and Japanese lanterns which were lining the shrubs and trees on the spacious lawn and croquet ground. The singing of Signor Pellico and of more than one amateur during the evening was greatly admired and after a few dances in the well

Government House, overlooking the new City Hall,
at the time of the Duke of Edinburgh's visit.

lighted central hall, the company separated at midnight, highly pleased with the royal Prince and with the hospitality of His Excellency the Governor.'

The VIP format – guard of honour, state banquet, reception, illuminated grounds, music (bar the contribution of the amateur vocalists), dancing and Chinese procession – was to continue unchanged at Government House into the 20th century.

The Duke and his party, besides fitting in formal engagements, cricket, bowls, Canton, Macau and theatricals, made an excursion up to Mountain Lodge and admired the view.

'His Royal Highness,' maintained the chaplain, whose sponsor wanted to get the Peak moving, 'expressed his surprise that the wealthy merchant princes of the colony had not yet availed themselves of the vicinity to their city of a position offering so bracing a climate, in the hottest time of the year. It is certainly difficult to account for the complete neglect of such a spot, as it takes only 50 minutes to reach it and less than 30 to return.'[1]

on the front porch of Government House.the Duke (third from right).

Government House from the north-east.

Typhoon trouble

MacDonnell's partiality for the Peak may have been helped along by his dislike of the hot and costly gas lighting down at Government House. It may also have had something to do with the white ants.

Right back in July 1841, the *Canton Press* had warned that white ants, thriving on humidity, would prove a formidable enemy to the new settlement. In 1853, Cleverly had described at some length how he had coated the timber of his Government House with coal tar and washed down the floors with arsenic in the hope of preventing the white ant/dry rot damage 'so common to almost all the buildings in the colony'.

By 1866, the year MacDonnell arrived, Cleverly's measures were ineffective: white ants had done so much damage that the wood-work of Government House had to have a complete overhaul. And by 1871, the roof was found to be entirely eaten through, necessitating its replacement.

Kennedy, taking over as Governor in April 1872, inherited the new roof and his predecessor's predilection for the Peak. After two summers, during one of which he had to put up the Grand Duke Alexis, son of the Tsar, down at Government House, he wrote home for permission to extend Mountain Lodge by two bedrooms, a sitting-room, and proper kitchen and servants' quarters.

'Having passed two hot seasons in Hong Kong without quitting my post,' he told the Secretary of State in October 1873, 'I feel assured that few persons can do so without imperilling their health (the capital of working men like myself) and it therefore becomes a question for consideration whether it is not more expedient and conducive to the welfare of the public service that the Governor should have a cottage affording the requisite change without periodically absenting himself from the colony and his work.'

Mountain Lodge and its outbuildings after the 1874 typhoon.

The estimate for the proposed extensions was rather high, he admitted, but this was purely because of the labour involved in carrying materials up the mountain and because of the need to build strongly against typhoons.[2]

Hong Kong and Britain were now linked by telegraph and Kennedy asked for prompt approval of his request so that some at least of the new facilities could be ready for use the following summer. A telegraph duly came in sanctioning the extensions and $9,000 was spent on them forthwith.

Then, in September 1874, the colony was hit by a monster typhoon that breached the sea wall, killed over 2,000 people and destroyed hundreds of houses and junks. Government House was undamaged ('beyond injury to a few venetians') but the newly-extended Mountain Lodge, reported the *Hong Kong Daily Press*, was 'completely unroofed, with the exception of one room. His Excellency the Governor and some ladies and gentlemen were at the Peak at the time and must have had a terrible night . . . The Governor's bungalow was purposely built in the strongest possible manner, and was considered to be proof against any typhoon that could occur.'[3]

A week later, the paper's attention returned to Government House over a court case concerning its chair-bearers. The Governor, coming down from the Peak as soon as the storm was over, had ordered three of them into Government House to sleep because he thought another typhoon was approaching. They had disobeyed, claiming they couldn't find a mat to sleep on.

Magistrate and newspaper were equally indignant. 'The defend-ants,' seethed the paper, 'further had the impudence to send into the Magistrate to state that they wished to go up to Government House and demand their wages.'[4]

Kennedy himself was no reactionary. He became the first Gover-nor of Hong Kong to open up functions at Government House to local people. The VIPs he entertained included the Hai Kwan of Canton and China's ambassador to Britain; and before he left the colony in 1877 a deputation of Chinese residents called at Govern-ment House to present him with a commemorative embroidered scroll.

Pope Hennessy

GOVERNMENT House and a restored Mountain Lodge now formed the backdrop to some remarkable years of entertainment and feud-ing, with John Pope Hennessy, the new Governor, making himself as unpopular with the Europeans as Kennedy had made himself popular with everyone.

Initially, all was calm enough. Sympathy may even have been on the new Governor's side since his Colonial Secretary was still on the Peak when he arrived and an hour late getting down to welcome him. 'To judge by the blundering hap-hazard manner in which so many of these state ceremonies have been carried out, in our experi-ence,' griped the *China Mail* on April 22, 1877, 'it is somewhat astonishing that we have succeeded in getting our administrators conveyed into Government House at all.'

Governor Hennessy and his young wife, Kitty.

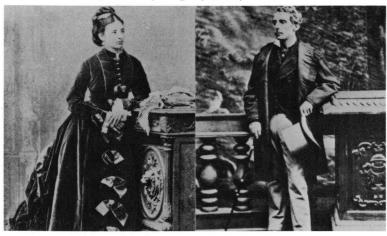

Hennessy, Irish like his three predecessors, brought with him his 26-year-old Eurasian wife Kitty and their young son. A week after their arrival, he gave a successful May Day levée at Government House for the men, while his wife held a reception on the lawns for the women. On May 24, he threw a ball for the Queen's birthday.

Like MacDonnell and Kennedy before him, however, he preferred to be at Mountain Lodge in high summer. By now the Peak was developing into the hill-station MacDonnell had envisaged. The Chief Justice and other leading expatriates had bungalows up there; and Hennessy, with a child of his own, was to comment that on children especially the change from the stagnant summer air of Victoria to fresh hill breezes had a markedly beneficial effect.

Sanitation, though, was a problem. Hennessy immediately claimed that the water supply was contaminated and he demanded an inspection of every Peak house, including his own. Thirteen houses were inspected. It was found that only three were using the dry earth system favoured by the Governor and that even Mountain Lodge provided no latrine for its hired labour.

Hennessy spelt out the improvements he required.

'From the evil consequences to my own health and another member of my household from using the water from the little valley N.E. of the Governor's Mountain Lodge,' he commented delicately in August 1877, 'I was convinced that what was called the Government sanitary station was a dangerous place to reside at . . . Looking to the injury my own health has already sustained by the flagrant neglect of sanitary arrangements in the vicinity of the Governor's Lodge – should any great delay occur in inducing the residents concerned to do what I now require, I shall be compelled to quit the lodge and, in spite of the inconvenience of removing at this season, to return to Government House.[5]

By 1879, household trouble of a different sort was brewing. On January 9, traveller Isabella Bird went to dinner at Government House with the Bishop. 'There were only,' she wrote in a letter, 'the Hennesseys, Major Palmer the ADC, and Mr Pitman consulting engineer of the Japanese Government. Mrs H. sat in a dream, spoke to no one and only roused herself to fire up fiercely at her husband who retorted with a cold sarcasm.'

The following day, the Governor withdrew an earlier recommendation of his that one Thomas Child Hayllar, QC, should be made Chief Justice. Years later the Governor's Private Secretary, E. J. Eitel, asserted that a suspicious Hennessy had returned unexpectedly to Government House from a projected launch trip to discover this Hayllar in his wife's boudoir, showing her an illustrated catalogue of indecent prints from a Naples museum. Hayllar had tried to hide the book. Hennessy had ordered Hayllar to get out of the house and take his book with him.

But no more was heard of Hayllar for the present. Hennessy was frenetically busy entertaining guests of his own. Always eager to please the Chinese community, he had started with a string of provincial officials from China. He now scored a hit with his hosting of Civil War hero General Grant, ex-President of the United States, who stopped at Hong Kong in May 1879 during a world tour.

'One of the children of our Queen has been residing in this house, and my immediate predecessor entertained here a son of the Emperor of Russia . . . but I believe,' exulted Hennessy at a Government House banquet given to Grant, 'the young princes would be themselves among the first to say that the man whose health I am now about to propose is the most illustrious guest that ever sat at this table.' The Governor's speech was printed verbatim in the Government Gazette.

Reception as usual followed banquet, and grounds as usual were illuminated. 'The American Star, a large design in gas, on the north side of Government House, was greatly admired,' commented the *China Mail* on May 5. 'The fairy-like beauty of the scene could scarcely have been enhanced. The lovely dresses of the ladies, the bright and varied uniforms of the officers of different nationalities present, laughter coming from various groups in the grounds, altogether made up a pleasing, lively and beautiful scene.'

The drawing-room of Government House in Hennessy's time.

A year later, when Prince Heinrich of Prussia was guest, no one was laughing.

The Governor had ordered a portrait of Albert, the late Prince Consort, to hang in the drawing-room of Government House. He invited Heinrich, as Albert's grandson, to assist at its unveiling and raised the Royal Standard of Prussia over the house. Again, the event was described at peculiar length in the Government Gazette, which even noted the melodies of the ancestral home of the Hohenzollerns played over lunch.

Hennessy then made the mistake of inviting Heinrich, a foreign national, to act as co-host at the state dinner to be given at Government House on the Queen's birthday. Major-General Donovan, the GOC, announced that he was giving a birthday dinner at Head Quarter House on the same day and that the only military band in the colony could not attend at Government House to play the national anthem. Hennessy protested. Donovan took no notice. Hennessy raised the matter with the executive council, claiming that Donovan was giving his dinner in deliberate opposition. Donovan, hearing this, became still more intransigent. Refusals began to arrive from those invited to the Government House dinner, including one from William Keswick of Jardine, Matheson. From Mountain Lodge, Hennessy cabled the Secretary of State. At the 11th hour, on May 23, Donovan called off his dinner.[6]

The King of Hawaii (centre front) with Hennessy, on his left.

From this point, Hennessy fought the European community all the way, with April 1881 marking the point of no return. Already, two years earlier, Isabella Bird had said that half the colony was not speaking to the other half and that the Governor was 'only on official speaking terms' with his executive council. Now Hennessy fell out publicly with Keswick, a member of the legislative council, over a visit to Hong Kong by King Kalakaua of Hawaii.

Keswick, in his Jardine capacity of Consul and agent for Hawaii, invited the King to stay at East Point. The Governor invited him to stay at Government House. The *China Mail* carried a story saying 'King Kalakaua will be offered the hospitality of Government House during his stay here; but it is not improbable that he will prefer to be the guest of Mr Keswick'.

On the King's arrival on April 12, there was a race out to his steamer during which, said Hennessy, the government officer bearing the formal Government House invitation was 'distanced by Mr Keswick'. Keswick advised the King to spend that night informally at East Point and proceed formally next day to Government House – at which point, Keswick maintained, Private Secretary Eitel threatened the King that he would go to Government House straight away or not at all.

Diplomatically, Kalakaua went straight to Government House. Equally diplomatically, he later expressed the hope that memories of his visit would not be disturbed by any controversy. Neither side listened and eventually the Secretary of State had to mediate.[7]

Kalakaua's visit impinged too on Hennessy's domestic problems. On April 20, Jardine's gave a garden party for the King at East Point. Hennessy did not attend but his wife did, and so did Hayllar. Photographer Afong took a picture of a group of guests which included the pair – a picture which Jardine managing partner F. B. Johnson, at the private request of Lady Hennessy, ordered him to suppress. A week later, on a public road, Hennessy laid about Hayllar with his umbrella.

The reverberations of this attack – described to the Secretary of State by Hayllar as a murderous, personal assault and by Hennessy as a brief, one-handed chastisement for an insult to 'a lady of my family' – were still echoing around the colony a year later when the Governor left it.

At one stage, when Hennessy was temporarily absent, Eitel invited Johnson to Government House to read the despatches relating to the attack and proceeded to discuss the earlier 'indecent prints' episode from which he said it stemmed. Hayllar, who was Jardine's legal adviser, started a $25,000 slander action against Eitel as a result; and Johnson, who was a member of the legislative council, requested a full inquiry.[8]

Midshipmen Albert Victor and George. To be received as Royal Navy.

The action was never brought and the inquiry was never held but it was into the atmosphere generated by such events that Victoria's teenage grandsons, Albert Victor and George (later George V) of Wales, sailed for Christmas 1881.

Orders came in that the boys, who were midshipmen on HMS *Bacchante,* were to be received only as Royal Navy not as Royal Family but an unabashed Hennessy had already laid on a ball in their honour. He gave it without them on December 22, throwing open the whole ground floor of Government House and putting up a supper-room in the grounds that was linked to the house by a covered way down the flight of steps. It was, gushed the *Hongkong Telegraph* despite the Hayllar scandal, 'probably the most brilliant and successful ball ever held at Government House.' The supper-room, erected around a large tree and with a central stove spreading warmth, was 'unique in its originality'.

Two days later, on Christmas Eve, the whole waterfront burst into colour for the princes. Government House, said the *Mail* in a 3½-column coverage of the illuminations, 'presented a really splendid appearance, the principal effect of which was observable from the water. The portion of the buildings to be seen from there was bright with the Gaelic motto "Cead Mille Failte" and above and on either side of the Prince of Wales' feathers were the initials of the young princes.'

A correspondent of the *Mail* was less impressed with the 'Cead Mille Failte' and the Governor who had had it put up:

'I say, Jinks, look at that 'ere Governor's 'ouse. Blank my eyes! "Good million frailties".'

'Whisht! Be aisy, me bhoy. That's the Oirish for a peerage and an extra thousand a year.'[9]

The boys lived on board throughout their stay but they called several times at Government House, having lunch there with the Governor and his wife on December 30, the day before they sailed, while a French band played on the verandah. That afternoon they walked to the top of the Peak, finding a good path the whole way.

'Went to the Governor's cottage,' they wrote in their journal, 'from which there are lovely views in either direction, down away to the islands south, as well as on the north side over Hong Kong roadstead, to Kowloon on the Chinese side of the strait, and to the mountains on the mainland. This afternoon it was perfectly clear.

'Looking eastward along the ridge from Victoria Peak to Mount Gough we were much surprised to find what a number of merchants' houses – we can count more than 50, each with its lawn-tennis court and racket court – have been built up there, on what a short time ago was a barren hill top with nothing but scrub and heather. There are admirable roads, and telephone and telegraphic communication with the town below, and they are talking of making a wire tramway up and down. The aspect of the hill has been entirely metamorphosed by all this planting, levelling, filling in with soil and turfing; it is now quite a second town up here.'[10]

7

Private architecture
(1883-1902)

ENNESSY'S sympathies had lain with the Asians and it was under
him that the first Chinese, Ng Choy, and the first Indian, E. R.
Belilios, joined the legislative council. In conventional expatriate
domesticity the Irishman expressed little interest, beyond approval
for moving up to the Peak in summer time. He was the first Governor
since Pottinger not to badger the Secretary of State about his residence and, although he was ready enough to spend money on entertaining VIPs, he called for no embellishments to either Government
House or Mountain Lodge.

In 1883, under Bowen, a modest wing was added to the lodge but
it was not until Des Voeux that there was any significant development
architecturally, and then the impetus came from residents rather than
the new Governor.

Des Voeux arrived in October 1887 and was sworn in at the council
chambers.

'I then proceeded,' he recalled in his memoirs,[1] 'to Government
House, which at once struck me as particularly convenient in design
and a model residence for a tropical climate. It was far superior,
indeed, as regards comfort, to other Government Houses of a more
pretentious character, which have been since built at much greater
cost . . . The roof was flat, and offered a magnificent view of the town
and harbour, thus permitting of agreeable exercise in illness or at
other times when seclusion was desirable. The grounds were not very
large, hardly exceeding two acres in extent, with flowering trees at
the sides. Beyond the offices and servants' quarters was another space
containing two asphalted lawn-tennis courts for use in rainy weather,
or at garden-parties when there were too many players for the other
three turf-courts . . .

'I found entertaining comparatively easy. The Chinese "com-
prador" and cook between them managed to provide in a wonderful
way for unexpected guests at extremely short notice, and the waiting
of the Chinese servants was exceptionally good. Rather different from
that of an English footman was their dress of long blue gowns, white
gaiters, thick Chinese shoes with white soles, and pigtails hanging
almost to the ground.'

A month after Des Voeux's arrival, Hong Kong celebrated Victoria's jubilee.

'On the morning of the celebration,' he wrote, 'the band of the
regiment and a large guard of honour marched into the grounds, and
my reception began. I "received" in the hall, the leading officials and
some 60 military and naval officers in uniform standing on either
side of me . . . Altogether, I shook hands with some 400 people.

'At five o'clock, attended by an escort of 12 Sikh mounted police,
I went down in my eight-coolie chair to review the troops. Three
other Government House chairs followed, the string of bearers look-

Governor Des Voeux. Agreed to a ballroom.

ing extremely well in their new bright-red liveries, white gaiters and "mutton-pie" hats with red tassels.

'The next day early the Chinese procession made its appearance at Government House, permission having been asked and readily given, for it to enter the grounds and pass my door. Having been misinformed as to its length, I had made an engagement for noon which I could not break and so, after watching the passing show from 10 to 12, I was obliged to leave for a time. When I returned at one, however, it was still passing, having been over $4\frac{1}{2}$ miles in length.'

The procession had contained more than 8,000 people.

Government House was being put to intensifying use, inside and out. In his first six months of office, Des Voeux estimated he had at least 400 people to lunch or dinner, besides those who came to dances and tennis parties.

'During this period, as indeed during all our winter seasons in Hong Kong,' he added, 'I had an almost continuous succession of guests staying in the house, among them being Mr George Curzon (now Lord Curzon, Viceroy of India).' By the time Des Voeux was forced to go off on sick leave in 1890, his list of house-guests had swelled to include Prince and Princess Henri de Bourbon, Russian Grand Duke Alexander Michael, Archduke Leopold of Austria and admirals, commodores and captains of the world's most powerful navies.

Such hospitality brought problems. Government House was by now nearly 40 years old. Considering the climate it had worn well, but it was not designed for entertaining on the scale that had become commonplace. There was no assembly room as such and large functions had to spill over into the Governor's private apartments and into the grounds, where arrangements were at the mercy of Hong Kong's volatile weather.

House-guest Princess Henri de Bourbon, Des Voeux and his daughter.

In 1887 when the jubilee programme was under discussion, someone had written to the *China Mail* deploring the lack of a ballroom at Government House and suggesting one should be added, called 'Victoria Hall'. Two years later, the legislative council voted for an extension to the house.

'Some of the members of Council,' wrote Des Voeux, 'having noticed that at our larger parties our rooms had become too small for the increased and increasing numbers of Hong Kong society, suggested to me the expediency of building an annexe to Government House, such as would afford greater space for balls, and would enable such entertainments to be given without disturbance to the Governor's domestic arrangements.

'I hesitated somewhat about the adoption of this suggestion, because of a doubt whether the Governor's salary was sufficient to render otherwise than inconvenient the amount of entertaining which the provision of such a building would cause to be expected. Seeing, however, that there was really a strong feeling on the subject and that, though the existing rooms at Government House were never by any means so crowded as are those of an ordinary London ball, their space was regarded as insufficient for comfort in a hot climate, I consented to the proposal in Council of the necessary vote.'

The project went through at speed. Government House proper had taken 10 years to get off the ground and four years to build. This 'annexe' to it, which turned out almost as large, was proposed one year, started the next and finished the next. Cleverly – still alive in England and drawing his Hong Kong pension – would have envied the Surveyor General of the day.

An expenditure was sanctioned of $40,000. Designs were drawn up by the private architectural firm of Palmer and Turner for a Victorian pile almost as tall as Cleverly's and linked to it by a covered stairway. These were approved by Des Voeux before he went on his sick leave in February 1890. A reception in March for the Duke and Duchess of Connaught 'sorely taxed the meagre accommodation of Government House', said the *China Mail*; and the annexe contract was let, to Yee Hing, almost as soon as the visitors were out of the door.

By July, the building was taking shape.

'The masonry is now advanced to 23 feet above the ground floor,' reported Surveyor General Samuel Brown, 'and the contractor is making good progress as the work suffers little interruption during rainy weather, owing to the protection afforded by a huge "matshed" which covers in the whole building.

'The new building will form a wing on the eastern side of Government House and will consist of a ballroom 60 feet long, 40 feet wide, and 26 feet high on the upper floor. It is approached from Government House by a vestibule and wide flight of steps. To the left is a billiard-room and on the right a staircase descends to the basement in which are placed a large supper-room, card and smoking rooms, and other conveniences.'[2]

The work was pushed on vigorously and on February 10, 1891, before even the contracted completion date, the annexe was used for a fancy-dress ball given by the Governor's wife as part of Hong Kong's own jubilee celebrations.

The ball, enthused the *Daily Press*, 'came off with much éclat. The figures 1841–1891 with the crown and V. R. on the gas standard at the entrance to the grounds, indicated that the function was associated with the colony's jubilee. Advantage was also taken of the occasion to open the handsome ballroom which has been built as an additional wing to Government House. The increased accommodation was, however, taxed to its utmost on Tuesday evening . . . There were about a hundred ladies present and more than twice as many gentlemen, and the scene in the ballroom with the mingling of colours and the numerous contrasts afforded by the fancy dresses and the consular, naval and military uniforms was one which will long remain in the memory . . . His Excellency the Governor, who wore his official uniform, and Lady Des Voeux, whose costume was that of 'A Swallow', moved freely about amongst their guests and contributed in every possible way to their enjoyment and happiness.

'Dancing was kept up with spirit until supper (served in the room below the ballroom), and was afterward resumed and continued until about half-past one.

Victoria in 1890. The ballroom, under construction

The house and its completed annexe

The house and its completed annexe

'The grounds of Government House and the facade had been hung with coloured lanterns, which produced a very pretty effect, and the floral decorations in the ballroom and on the staircase were much admired.'

A couple of months later, Nicholas, future Tsar and Emperor of All the Russias, sailed into Hong Kong to be greeted by a 450-gun cannonade and the Governor in his phaeton at the wharf. The Tsarevich rode with Des Voeux up to Government House where he stayed an hour or so, professing himself delighted with the view from its roof and deriving great amusement, wrote Des Voeux, 'from watching through a high-power telescope the doings upon his ship some half a mile away'.

That August, there was a wedding from the house. Major-General Barker was Acting Governor and Helena, his eldest daughter, married Assistant Colonial Secretary F. H. May. After the wedding, said the *Daily Press*, the couple were 'mendelssohned' out of the Cathedral and driven to Government House where a huge wedding-cake set up in the new ballroom was cut and distributed to guests.

Hong Kong hill-station

HIGH summer remained a problem. Government House now offered much more room but, since the acquisition of Mountain Lodge back in 1867, Hong Kong's governors had tended to find life from May to September too hot down in the town.

Mountain Lodge though, despite its romantic, tucked-away site at the top of Hong Kong, was a poor residence compared with the merchants' villas that had gone up on the Peak since. It was so small, remembered Des Voeux, that it permitted little entertainment beyond garden-parties around its two grass tennis-courts; and in 1888, during his first summer there, it was invaded by white ants.

'What was, however, far more trying to patience on the Peak was the time when clouds rested upon it. In our first year this happened but rarely, and never lasted more than a day or two. But in our second season it was very different, and this miserable experience lasted for the greater part of the summer. On one occasion, for several weeks together, the fog was as dense as the worst which afflicts London in November, and only differed from it as being white instead of brown or black. The damp inside the house was such that water ran down the walls in streams and collected in pools on the polished floors. Such indeed was the moisture of the air that bed linen had to be kept in a hot drying-room, and would become too wet to sleep in if it was taken out more than a few minutes before it was required to be used. At such times one seemed cut off entirely from the rest of the world, the existence of which was revealed only at rare intervals by the arrival of a government messenger with papers, or by the clicking of the telephone.

'When this was the state of the atmosphere with us, the heat in the town below was usually at its greatest, and yet in going down to my office, as I used to do once or twice a week, I found it a welcome change. Occasionally, after many days in succession of a life which resembled that of a damp and gloomy prison, we would go for a change down to sleep for a night or two at our house in town. It was a pleasure to see daylight and bright sky again, but the heat, which rendered sleep almost impossible, quickly drove us up again.'

Council was largely sympathetic. When in 1890 it voted the $40,000 for a Government House annexe, it voted another $40,000 for a more substantial Governor's residence on the Peak which, following Des Voeux's bill of 1888 reserving it to housing on the European model and since the opening the same year of the Peak tramway, had become enormously desirable to expatriates.

The Government House annexe had been achieved very quickly. Mountain Lodge Mark III took as long as Cleverly's mansion to get off the ground. Des Voeux did not push for its completion. There was a huge programme of public works in hand, including the grand praya reclamation scheme launched by the Duke of Connaught, and some unofficial members of the council were complaining. When ill-health obliged Des Voeux to give up his governorship in 1891, the lodge was virtually abandoned to the white ants.

'The present condition of Mountain Lodge is most unsatisfactory,' reported Acting Surveyor General Francis Cooper. 'The buildings were erected some years ago, before residence in the Hill District assumed anything like the proportions it has of recent years, and are now in a delapidated condition and practically unfit for occupation.'[3]

The $40,000 stayed on the books and 'Craigieburn', a gas-lit, eight-bedroom former hotel on Plantation Road, was rented in 1892 for Governor Sir William Robinson, 'at a rent of $1,500 for the season'.[4]

At the close of that season, Robinson sent home plans by Cooper (now Director of Public Works) for a new, two-storey house costing $62,000 on a site just above the existing Mountain Lodge. With them went a despatch that Governor Bonham might have dictated.

'The existing house, apart from the fact of its being beyond repair,' Robinson declared, 'is a mere bungalow, quite inadequate to hold an ordinary-sized family, and affording very insufficient accommodation for the large staff of servants which the Governor has to keep (the chair bearers alone in my employ number no less than 18) and no room at all for the reception of the increasing number of distinguished visitors who pass through the colony.

'The house designed by Mr Cooper is by no means on an extravagant scale and it will afford no more accommodation than is reasonably necessary. It is a house in the same style, though naturally somewhat larger, as local residents now build for themselves in place of the bungalows which formerly served the purpose of residences during the finer months of the summer only.'[5]

And Bonham would have found the tone of the Secretary of State's reply familiar, too. Defer any such outlay, wrote the Marquis of Ripon early in 1893, until you have sorted out your estimates.

The vote now not only had to be kept on the books but also increased to match Cooper's estimate. In the summer of 1893, by when two ceilings at Mountain Lodge had caved in and the Craigieburn rent had gone up to $2,400, the matter was debated at length in a council meeting.

Craigieburn was quite inadequate for his staff of 40, maintained Governor Robinson. 'It is certainly quite impossible to put up archdukes, foreign admirals and the numerous distinguished visitors who are constantly arriving.'

Unofficial member E. R. Belilios, who had a house adjoining Mountain Lodge, believed the colony could afford to start building a new lodge immediately and made an impassioned plea for hill-stations and the Peak in general, and for the site of Mountain Lodge in particular. Unofficials Paul Chater, the financier, and T. H. Whitehead, manager of the Chartered Bank, said the time was not right for such expenditure, that for instance the colony's stamp and opium revenues were currently in jeopardy. Whitehead further described Mountain Lodge as an outlandish, out-of-the-way place...

'In the time of His Excellency Sir William Des Voeux, on three or four different occasions within two or three weeks, out of dinner parties consisting of from 18 to 24, no one turned up; and once or twice only one or two guests of that number were able to appear. The road to Mountain Lodge on a dark night is a very dangerous one and in stormy weather particularly.'

Whitehead accused Belilios of pushing the project because it would increase the value of his own property.

A motion was finally passed that $60,000 should be spent on a new Peak residence for the Governor when funds were readily available.[6]

One month later, the Governor addressed the finance committee from Craigieburn. He needed a supplementary furniture vote, he wrote, because he had had to buy items for the two best bedrooms to make them fit for guests. 'When the two bedsteads in these bedrooms were sold,' he explained to the committee's merriment, 'they only fetched between them $5.'

The following year plague hit Hong Kong, the Sino-Japanese War broke out, Lady Robinson died up at Craigieburn – and new summer homes were off the agenda.

In 1897 what remained of Mountain Lodge was pulled down. The lease on Craigieburn expired and one was taken from January 1898 on 'The Cliffs', a four-bedroom oil-lit house owned by Chater further down Plantation Road.[7] As this was the only 'tolerably suitable' house on offer and the rent was $2,600, the question of rebuilding Mountain Lodge was revived at a council meeting in March 1899. By now, the estimated cost of the project had risen to $75,000.

Sir Henry Blake, new to the job of Governor, decided to wait at least one summer before determining the site of the lodge, 'because

A commodious new Mountain Lodge on spectular hilltop . . .

I think,' he said, 'it is my duty not alone to consult my own convenience in this matter but to look forward a little and consider the possible expansion of the colony and possible best position for future Governors.'[8]

If he had the newly-leased New Territories in mind as a site, he did not say so. And when he toured them August, he found so much robbery and piracy that he had to increase the strength of the police and water-police all round. There was no question yet of locating any country residence for the Governor out there.

In October, Blake told London that the Mountain Lodge site approved by Robinson in 1892 seemed on the whole the most suitable and that, as the colony's finances were in good shape, site preparation was proceeding. Cooper's plans, however, he disliked, and Palmer and Turner had been asked to prepare fresh ones for a larger, more tasteful house. This had been done and the firm hoped a contractor could be found to build their house for the $75,000 that had been voted.[9]

In 1900, a $97,000 contract was let to Sang Lee by the Public Works Department for a house it prophesied would be 'the largest and handsomest building at the Peak'.

Work began on what proved to be a turreted Victorian grange complete with balustered staircase, billiard-room, school-room, seven bedrooms, panelled dadoes, fireplaces, gas lighting, tessellated verandahs, and a lightning conductor on each of its four towers.

In September 1902, Blake and his family moved into a commodious new Mountain Lodge that stood in 43 acres of spectacular hilltop and was approached via a small gate-lodge up a drive cutting through $2\frac{1}{2}$ acres of garden and pleasure ground.[10]

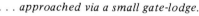

. . . approached via a small gate-lodge.

8   Change of role
(1903-25)

THE annexe to Government House had electricity and so, from the turn of the century, had the main building. For both Victoria's diamond jubilee in 1897 and her son's coronation in 1902, the crown decorating Government House was done in electric light bulbs.

In 1908, when Hongkong Electric followed up by installing 42 electric fans, summer on Upper Albert Road suddenly became bearable.

The new Mountain Lodge had at first only gas; and it was as difficult to reach as its fore-runners. The Peak tram, with its front seat reserved for the Governor, had cut the journey to the top of Victoria Gap to 10 minutes but from there – unless, like Belilios, you imported a camel – it was still a long, steep haul by sedan-chair. On top of this there was the damnable mist which occasionally, as Des Voeux had complained, persisted right through the summer, plus the sheer expense of living up a mountain where, as he once reported to London, every brick and stone, every piece of timber and stick of furniture had to be carried on men's shoulders for distances of up to two miles.[1]

For the comparative coolness, it had been considered worth it. The view from the south-west verandah across the South China Sea was magnificent – better, arguably, even than that from the 100 or so other houses now perched up in the Hill District – but it was the coolness that really justified the time, effort and money.

The introduction of electric fans down in the town changed all that. Mountain Lodge became not so much an essential alternative to Government House through the heat of summer as merely a good one when the weather did not happen to be too humid.

For its first few years, however, the lodge was used more or less as its council supporters had envisaged, although the number of summer visitors wanting a bed was rather fewer than had been indicated.

Blake departed in 1903 and Nathan was due to arrive in July 1904. During the interregnum, while May was Acting Governor, a bill was passed reserving residence on the Peak not merely for those with European-style housing but for expatriates as such. Those from temperate climates suffered, the bill's protagonists claimed, when forced to live in the lower levels of tropical places and they were in danger of being crowded out up the mountain.[2]

'Kindly telegraph me the word "Peak",' wrote May to Nathan, 'if you desire that arrangements be made for your occupying on your arrival your Peak residence . . . It is ever so much cooler and healthier than Government House at this season of the year.'

Nathan, a bachelor, made friendly use of Mountain Lodge. Three weeks after his arrival, he gave a party on its lawns for 80 children,

Governor Lugard hosting representatives
of the Chinese Navy.

providing a band and toboggan slide and distributing presents from a Governor's post office. Some of his Hong Kong colleagues – Major-General Hatton, Chief Justice Piggott and their wives – Nathan allowed to stay up there for protracted periods, with or without him.

'You have no idea what the nights are here – I am half dead,' Emily Hatton wrote to Nathan once from Head Quarter House, just before moving up to the lodge with her husband. Such-and-such a woman has been commenting, she wrote him again after returning to the heat of the town, 'about the length of our stay at Mountain Lodge. I hear she thinks me a designing woman . . . how I wish we were dining with you *en famille* at Mountain Lodge tonight.'[3]

Lugard, when he arrived in July 1907 to succeed Nathan, went straight to Mountain Lodge by chair and Peak tram.

'After the train journey which lasted only a few minutes,' wrote his journalist wife Flora next day to her brother-in-law Edward, 'there were still more chairs and more scarlet-clad bearers to carry us up and up round the sides of the rocky but flower-covered hills, through pure air which grew cooler every moment across little dips and cuttings each giving us a more exquisite view than the last of seas and islands, till finally we were marched abreast through the gates of Government House' (Mountain Lodge in this context) 'to find ourselves in a beautifully kept English garden with shaven lawns, tennis courts and flowering shrubs and to be deposited at the foot of the steps leading up under a stone porch to a cool brown wood hall where the house-servants drawn up on either side were awaiting their new masters.'

They arrived on a good day. Even so, Lugard of Africa had reservations. 'Mountain Lodge,' he informed his brother by the same post, 'is exquisitely situated with views of green islands set in a blue sea far below. But it is dreadfully damp, worse than Nigeria in the rains, envelopes all glued together, cigars like bits of sponge.'

Government House proper, however, he thought splendid; and his wife, once she had done some prettifying, called it 'charming now – like a comfortable English country house'. The pair used it to the limit.

The week he arrived, Lugard held a big initial levée, 'and wagged my head . . . till I felt like a Chinese image on a mantelpiece'. By the end of September, he and his wife had established a routine of fortnightly dinner parties at Government House for up to 40 people and at Mountain Lodge for up to 20.

In November, taxing even the ballroom that had 'ample space for at least 12 sets of quadrilles', the couple gave a King's birthday ball for 1,000 guests.

'I have to open the State Lancers,' wrote the Governor to his

Viceroy Chang Jen-chun at Government House. Lugard sits next to him.

brother, 'I must go and see that I know how it is to be done . . . I thought the entertainment and function business here was pretty scorching but now that the cold weather is coming on it is warming up with a vengeance!

'Flora has made a simply wonderful bunderbuss for this ball. She has very large ideas, – has had a huge staircase some 12 foot broad and with a huge half way landing constructed outside from the ball room to the garden, domed over with arches and all lit up by electric light.'[4]

That year, the last before electric fans, the Lugards did not move down from Mountain Lodge to Government House until the end of November. Thereafter, use of the lodge that 15 years earlier had been deemed 'an absolute necessity', depended on the tastes of individual governors. Some liked it hot. Some didn't.

But the lodge had at least one famous guest, in the person of Kitchener of Khartoum. Kitchener arrived in Hong Kong in September 1909 on a retirement tour, was 'tickled to death' at the sight of the Government House sedans and got into his the wrong way round. He rode up to Mountain Lodge, came down to Government House for dinner, and returned to the Peak to sleep. Next day, he wandered the grounds of Mountain Lodge until tiffin time, then departed for Canton.[5]

Down on Upper Albert Road, hospitality worked itself to a climax. Nathan had put up, among other royal travellers, Prince Fushimi, Japan's highest prince of the blood. Lugard, for his part, twice welcomed China's Viceroy Chang Jen-chun to a full official luncheon; and he followed up his 1907 King's birthday ball with equally large and brilliant ones in 1908 and 1909.

In the winter of 1910–11 came, as Lugard put it, 'a plethora of princes', plus Mrs George Keppel 'who entirely ran King Edward VII for the last 10 or 12 years'.

And on June 22, 1911, George V was crowned. Lugard, linking the grounds of Government House with those of the public gardens opposite, threw a reception for anybody and everybody in the colony who wished to attend, just so long as they wore evening-dress.

'It is estimated,' said the *China Mail*, 'that some 6,000 residents of all nationalities were present. Everybody had a right royal time of it . . .

'On arrival the guests lined up at the main entrance to Government House and at 8.30 pm began to move into the palatial residence. His Excellency the Governor took up a position in the hall and as the guests passed through into the grounds on the northern side of the building he personally shook hands with each one and welcomed all with a brief word and a cheery smile . . . On the northern face of Government House itself were a number of sparkling electric light devices, comprising the crown, the letters 'G.R.' and the Prince of Wales' plumes. Strings of Japanese lanterns outlined the pathway to the public gardens, which were specially connected with Government House grounds for the occasion. Here the sight was one of enchanting beauty, altogether surpassing description. It was like fairyland.'

It was also the biggest function ever held at Government House. His predecessors' celebrations of Victoria's jubilees, of Hong Kong's jubilee, of Edward VII's coronation – none of them touched for sheer size Lugard's 1911 celebration for George V.

War and peace

DIFFERENT, more demanding times were ahead.

In October 1911, the same month that saw the first through train from Kowloon to Canton, China rose against the Manchu dynasty, establishing a republic.

In Hong Kong, in 1912, May became Governor and was nearly assassinated during his inaugural procession to City Hall and Government House, by a bullet that lodged in Helena May's sedan-chair.

World War I broke out, the regulars left to fight and Hong Kong's

Volunteer Corps took over the defence of a colony that now had half a million people.

'One became accustomed to the sight of men going to their offices, to the club, to social functions in full battle-order.' recalled a member of the corps. 'I remember attending a soirée at Government House and leaving my rifle and equipment in the cloak-room before going in to shake hands with Sir Henry and Lady May. I would like to be able to say that I had danced at Government House in shorts and ammunition boots; I was dared to, but lacked the moral courage.'[6]

The Germans never came but China signed Japan's Twenty-one Demands and the writing was on the wall. By the peace celebrations of summer 1919, the old order had changed even in Hong Kong. A reception was held at Government House but the house was no longer the inevitable focal-point of celebrations.

The Governor's salary was now £6,000 – the same, curiously, as it had been back at the beginning of the colony when the man at the helm was also Plenipotentiary and Superintendent of Trade – but from May's time, the Blue Books defined the sum as £4,800 salary and £1,200 'entertainment allowance'. Coincidence or not, entertainment at Government House was never again quite so extravagant.

Stubbs succeeded May when peace came, and Mountain Lodge was scarcely used.

'It was by far the best house on the Peak', recalls Stubbs' ADC, now Major-General Sir Robert Neville, 'but it was always shrouded in mist and the last part still had to be done by chair. You couldn't take a car up, you couldn't even take a car over Wan Chai Gap so you couldn't entertain up there properly because of the problem of guests getting there and back. Anyway, the drawing and dining rooms weren't as big as at Government House; and there was no ballroom.'

Stubbs disliked the lodge so much in fact, says Neville, that he probably stayed up there only once or twice.

'If you'd been able to drive up, we might have gone there for weekends but, why bother? Government House was beautifully cool; it always had lots of windows; there was plenty of ice; and by then it was all overhead fans, no punkahs at all.'

At Mountain Lodge, the white ants had moved in but Government House seemed to be in top condition – a white, stuccoed building with cool dark shutters at its windows and heavy dark furniture within. The link between Cleverly's mansion and the Palmer and Turner annexe was still only a covered flight of steps but the two were regarded as a single building.

Outside, the south-facing lawn immediately in front of the house was marked out for tennis, and two umbrella trees with slatted seats at the base shaded the pillared porte-cochère. Neville's string of polo ponies was stabled in part of the block that had once housed the Governor's carriage and race-horses. The rest of the block was knocked down to make way for garages and staff quarters.

On the north bank, azaleas were planted for the first time. 'It was my idea,' says Neville. 'I'd been up to Japan and seen the azaleas there. I thought what a mass of colour they would be at Government House, seen from the harbour.'

Year-round entertainment at Government House centred on formal weekly dinners and informal tennis-parties. The King's birthday celebrations had been pared down, as far as Government House was concerned, to a morning reception where 200 or so people filed past the Governor standing on a dais in the ballroom ('and in those days, the girls all bobbed to him'), followed by an afternoon garden-party with a more extensive invitation list.

Guests at the house during Stubbs' time included Anna Pavlova, who danced at the City Hall. But the star performer, in Hong Kong's opinion, was Edward Prince of Wales (later Edward VIII) who arrived for a couple of days on April 6, 1922 – shortly after a sea-men's strike that had, unthinkably, spread to include domestic servants and left Government House with only two Hakka staff.

'Neither Stubbs nor I had any experience of royal visits,' says

The ADC's polo ponies, stabled in front of the ballroom.

The Prince of Wales at Government house in 1922, with Stubbs.

Neville, 'so we telegrammed Mountbatten, the Prince's equerry who was coming with him, asking for advice. The reply came back that the Prince would like to play polo (I lent him my best polo pony) and that he hated long dinner parties so could we please make the banquet not more than four courses.

'We compromised on six courses. The ballroom seated 120 for dinner, with the Prince at the top table on the dais. I saw him look at his watch halfway through, then pull out his cigarettes.

' "Excuse me, Sir," Stubbs said, "but you're surely not going to smoke before your father's health is drunk?"

' "Well, either I am," he replied, "or we're going to drink his health now." So the port was passed around before the roast beef.'

It had been a day of exaggerations. On landing that morning, Edward had warily taken the Government House sedan from the pier to Upper Albert Road 'through streets packed with Chinese who made not a murmur. It was a mark of respect,' comments Neville who marched alongside, 'but most embarrassing for us.'

At Government House, the contrast was total. The Prince inspected the guard of honour at the gates and passed through on to the lawns. At the sound of a whistle, out to greet him from their hiding places in the surrounding shrubberies, reported the *Mail*, 'sprang a horde of boy scouts and girl guides, all yelling shrilly'.

9 Town and country
(1926-41)

IN 1926, shortly after Clementi took over as Governor, the wealthy Sir Paul Chater died, bequeathing Hong Kong his huge collection of historical pictures, books and porcelain.

All those pictures that were not already hung, Clementi inspected at Government House. It was decided that most of the oils, water-colours and ink sketches would grace the Governor's residence and Hong Kong University while the remaining items, largely prints, would be allocated to government offices. Ten of the 400 pictures in the collection were original oils and drawings by George Chinnery.[1] For the first time, Government House had some good paintings to hang alongside its standard royal portraits.

Cleverly's mansion had by this stage been occupied for 70 years. Its roof had been replaced, the Palmer and Turner annexe had been added, out-buildings had changed but essentially the old house was intact.

Now it was decided to join it more firmly to its annexe, enlarging the ballroom at the same time.

Sang Lee were again called in, to do a job that included lengthening the ballroom to the east and making a conservatory with a faun's-head fountain in front of the steps linking house and annexe. The ornamental plaster-work of the ballroom ceiling needed renewing and when work on it started, the pitched roof was found to be so riddled with white ants and dry rot that it had to be replaced by a flat one of steel and concrete. This, by the addition of stairs and ornamental bronze lamps, was turned into a roof-garden while the south verandah was incorporated into the ballroom to enlarge it still further.

The whole job, done in 1929, cost $152,000.[2]

Up at Mountain Lodge, though the gardens were lush and lovely, white ants were playing similar havoc. In Stubbs' day, several floors had had to be renewed because of them and by the 1930s, the timber of the lodge was needing treatment every year.

Suddenly in 1932, when Peel was in office, it was suggested that the Governor should have a retreat at Fanling instead of on Victoria Peak, plus a brand-new Government House arising out of a multi-million-dollar urban renewal scheme.

Hong Kong was at that stage considered to be weathering the Great Depression rather better than the rest of the world; and Japan's sensational seizure of Manchuria was disregarded.

'As regards His Excellency the Governor's proposed retreat in the New Territories, I heartily support it,' declared unofficial W. E. L. Shenton when the legislative council debated the estimates in which it featured, 'especially as it is bound up with the abandonment of Mountain Lodge and the building of a new official residence on the Island. Mountain Lodge has been distasteful to numerous

Clementi with Chiang Kai-shek's Marshal Li, 1928

governors, as it cuts them off from the colony's administration. To those who have to attend on His Excellency during the summer months, it takes up a large part of a business day.

'The present Government House is fast falling into decay and the report on the state of the roof of the ballroom when it was found to be in a very dangerous condition is still fresh in our memory.

'I have called for the figures to show what government money has been spent in recent years on Mountain Lodge and Government House, and I am informed that since 1928 $35,532 has been spent on Mountain Lodge and $190,887 on Government House. I think everyone will agree with me that the foregoing shows that these two buildings are not today economic propositions. I am also informed that extensive repairs are again being carried out at Government House.

'The Governor, in my opinion, needs a retreat from the cares and worries of his official position, in addition to which our New Territories are assuming every year a greater and greater importance and the presence of His Excellency there will, I feel sure, be not only much appreciated but also of benefit to the colony.'

'The support given by the council to this proposal,' replied Acting Governor Southorn, 'will be very gratifying to His Excellency Sir William Peel who has authorised me to say that when a new Government House, on a cooler site, is ready for occupation – as we hope it soon may be, for the present Government House which was built in 1852 is seldom free from workmen – His Excellency is prepared to relinquish Mountain Lodge as a Governor's residence.'[3]

Southorn (centre): 'The Governor needs a retreat.'

'The house has become intolerably noisy.'

The Government House which would permit Mountain Lodge to be abandoned after only 30 years of use was itself to be on the Peak. The site selected was at Magazine Gap and, like that of the lodge, was a picturesque one that the military had originally tried as a sanatorium and rejected as unhealthy.[4]

The existing Government House was to be given up and the site sold as part of a scheme to sell off or redevelop all the government sites enclosed by Upper Albert Road/Ice House Street/Queen's Road/Garden Road, and to build new government offices and a new City Hall within the area.

'There are two main reasons for the abandonment of the present house and site,' Colonial Secretary D. W. Tratman explained to the council in September 1933, 'the first being that, apart from the ballroom, the structure of the present house is worn out and large sums are being expended to keep it in repair – the accommodation, it may be added, being hopelessly inadequate.

'The second reason is that with the growth of motor traffic on the hilly roads which surround it, the house has become intolerably noisy.

'Another factor in the case is the development scheme on the plan before you. Even if it were desirable to leave the present site of Government House untouched, the scheme involves new buildings which must detract considerably from such amenities as the site still enjoys.

Fanling Lodge, two miles from China

'Then we have the problem of Mountain Lodge. No one, I think, will deny that it is very inaccessible and therefore inconvenient according to modern ideas of communication. Moreover, despite the provision of central heating, the house cannot be described as pleasant to live in in the months when it should be a real relief to the Governor and his family from the stuffiness of the lower levels.

'The new site therefore needs to be lower than Mountain Lodge and higher than the present site, also quieter. All these considerations are met by the Magazine Gap site.'[5]

The Government House and City Development Scheme needed special sanction by the Secretary of State. The proposed retreat at Fanling was independent of the scheme and went through without more ado. This time, the government did not look outside for an architect but used designs by S. C. Feltham of the Public Works Department. Construction began that same year of an elegant white lodge standing on low ground adjoining the new Fanling Golf Course, only a couple of miles from the China border. And in 1934 Fanling Lodge was finished: a two-storey country house with five bedrooms for $140,000.[6]

Now the Governor of Hong Kong had three residences – one in the city, one in the country and one up a mountain. Mountain Lodge was not relinquished as intended, because the City Development Scheme ran into trouble.

Financially the scheme was meant to be self-sustaining, drawing its funds from the sale of some of the government sites embraced by it, but by 1934 the bottom had dropped out of the market even in Hong Kong.

'The trade depression hangs very heavily on us,' admitted Peel that September. 'In view of the state of the property market in Hong Kong today, it is possible that the scheme will take longer to complete than was originally anticipated.'[7]

An approach road to the proposed $2 million house at Magazine Gap was finished in 1935 and there that part of the scheme was left since the depression persisted and since Caldecott, who succeeded Peel, disliked the idea of intensive development around Albert Road and remained unconvinced of the need for a new Government House.

Northcote succeeded Caldecott and agreed, so far as a new Government House was concerned, with Peel.

'I consider,' he declared in a paper written to lay before the legislative council on October 13, 1938, 'that the project of moving Government House to another site should be proceeded with at once, both on economic grounds and as an essential preliminary to a worthy development of the area lying between Queen's Road and the public gardens.'

Cost of the Magazine Gap house was estimated at $2 million. Sale of the existing Government House site (at $8 per square foot) would raise $1.2 million of this but was not essential since sale of some of the other sites included in the redevelopment scheme would bring in more than enough money. Hong Kong's economy had picked up dramatically, thanks in large part to a population that had soared as a result of continuing Sino-Japanese hostilities.

By the time the council actually met that October 13, however, Japanese forces had invaded South China's Kwangtung province. That night, heavy gunfire was heard from the Pearl River delta. A week later, Canton fell.

Dragon-dance on the lawn. George V's Silver Jubilee, 1935

Japan's move

JAPAN had been moving in on China since the end of the 19th century.

Chiang Kai-shek established a National government on the mainland in 1928 – his Marshal Li Chai-sum arrived in Hong Kong by gunboat and stayed with Clementi at Government House – but was initially too engrossed with civil war to stop foreign encroachment. Since 1931, and more particularly since 1937 when the encroachment changed to full-scale (though still undeclared) invasion, Japan had worked her way down from the north until now her army had arrived 90 miles away at Canton.

Government House continued to celebrate royal jubilees and accessions and birthdays as it had for nearly a century.

On October 27, 1938, five days after the fall of Canton, one Major Matsutani of the Japanese Imperial Army came from there by trawler 'solely for the purpose of paying respect to His Excellency the Governor of Hong Kong and their Excellencies the Highest Commanders of the Royal Navy and Army on behalf of the Japanese military authorities in South China'.

The same *China Mail* that carried a report of his press conference – a conference at which Matsutani was questioned on the possibility of Japan's extending operations in the direction of Hong Kong – carried a notice about two forthcoming dances at Government House. 'Chauffeur-driven cars will park on Murray Parade Ground where a special telephone to Government House will be installed . . . Sedan chairs and rickshaws will set down their passengers at the main entrance to Government House in Upper Albert Road.'

The following week, the legislative council agreed to $100,000 being spent on levelling the site for a Government House at Magazine Gap.

In 1939, although the City Development Scheme as such was scrapped, plans were drawn up for the new house. Again by Feltham, they were for a terraced 'Mediterranean' building with 18 bedrooms, on a spur of land overlooking the Aberdeen valley and Lamma Island. A formal Italian garden with a stone pergola would lead to broad lawns merging into the steep hillside. The ground floor of the house would incorporate the requisite ballroom and billiard room. The basement would incorporate an air-raid shelter.

On August 17, a contract was let for constructing the foundations. Three weeks later, it was cancelled.[8] Britain had declared war on Germany.

It was still two years before the inevitable happened, two years during which Hong Kong spent heavily on air-raid precautions and a ladies' working party was held three times a week at Government

House to aid the British war effort.

In the summer of 1940, British wives and children were evacuated to Australia and Hong Kong acquired a military Governor, Lt-General E. F. Norton, who stood in for Northcote at Government House and saw the colony through its subdued centenary in January 1941.

Northcote returned in March 1941, broadcasting a message to the colony from George VI and presiding over the King's birthday celebrations in June. Since the outbreak of war, these had been confined to a military parade followed by a consular corps reception at Government House. Northcote, who was ill, was obliged to make 1941's reception informal, and apologised for it.

'I am afraid,' he told the consuls, 'that I myself am a little like my poor house at the present moment: that is to say, not in very good repair.'[9]

The cold truth was that Government House was falling down. Everyone knew it and a song of the day, sung to the tune of 'London Bridge is falling down', blamed Wing-Commander Steele-Perkins, Hong Kong's new Director of Air-raid Precautions. An air-raid tunnel, driven underneath the house, had so disturbed its foundations that the walls had had to be shored up with great timbers . . . The maligned Mountain Lodge might have to be used in earnest and suddenly some money was spent on alterations and improvements to it.

On September 10, Sir Mark Young arrived to replace Northcote and broadcast from Government House an immediate appeal to Hong Kong to play its part 'whether war itself comes to our waters or our shores, or whether it remains far off'. To the protesting 'bachelor husbands', he pointed out that he had left his wife and daughter behind.

In November, following reports that 50,000 Japanese troops had massed around Canton, he appealed from Government House for more civil defence recruits. Hong Kong's population was now 1.6 million, nearly doubled in five years by refugees from China.

On December 2, the Governor and Hong Kong society in general attended Sir Robert and Lady Ho Tung's lavish diamond wedding celebration at the Hong Kong Hotel.

On December 7, following a report from Fanling to Major-General Maltby that the Japanese were mustering near the border, Young as Governor and Commander-in-Chief put the colony on a war footing, mobilising all forces. On December 8, Japan bombed Pearl Harbour – and attacked Hong Kong, wiping out the little airfield at Kai Tak.

By December 13, the day Guam fell, all Maltby's troops had been forced back on to Hong Kong Island. From Upper Albert Road,

Young rejected two Japanese demands for surrender that were conveyed by launch across the harbour.

'I was called to Government House at one point to take orders about my engineers,' remembers Sir Lawrence Kadoorie, who had already been directed to blow up the generating station of his China Light and Power Company. 'I went in at the tunnel entrance on Lower Albert Road, up three flights of steps to the top where I found the Governor and the army people who had descended from the house. The phones weren't working – they had been shelled or something – so there was the Government of·Hong Kong, cut off in a cave.'

Kadoorie was not the only one called to Government House in odd circumstances. Captain Batty-Smith, the Governor's ADC, called in Thomas Harmon, PWD's Inspector of Furniture, and a Hungarian picture-restorer by the name of Von Kobza Nagy,

Sir Mark Young. From Government House to the Peninsula

apparently to discuss concealment at Government House of the more valuable pictures from the Chater collection.[10]

It was a risky hiding-place to choose. Canossa Hospital above Government House was destroyed by Japanese bombing. The cathedral and Government Offices below Government House were hit. The Peak was heavily shelled and bombed.

From London, Winston Churchill sent the Governor a message saying every day that Hong Kong held out was of value to the Allies.

On Christmas Eve, with Japanese troops overrunning much of the Island, greetings were sent out to surviving fighting units from Government House and from Fortress HQ cut deep into the hill behind Flagstaff House.

At 3.15 pm on Christmas Day, Maltby advised Young that no further military resistance was feasible. The white flag was flown over Government House and that evening Young and Maltby crossed the harbour to Kadoorie's Peninsula Hotel to surrender the colony in person to Lt-General Takashi Sakai, Commander-in-Chief of the Japanese forces in South China.

The house Fujimura built
(1942-45)

THE unbelievable had happened and Hong Kong had a Japanese general as its Governor – not Sakai, headquartered in the Peninsula Hotel, but China expert Lt-General Rensuke Isogai, a former Chief-of-Staff of the Japanese Kwantung Army, who arrived two months after the colony's surrender.

Sir Mark Young was a prisoner-of-war and by the beginning of 1942 all his former staff had been moved down to Prince's Building. The *Hongkong News*, Japan's instant English-language propaganda paper, made it clear that there was 'not the least possibility of a British official being appointed as Governor, and it fell to Colonial Secretary F. C. Gimson – who had arrived to take up his post only the day before Japan attacked – to hand over the administration.

The Hongkong and Shanghai Bank on Des Voeux Road was selected as the headquarters of the Japanese civil administration and Gimson, along with 2,500 other Allied civilians, went off to internment at Stanley.

On February 20 – by when Manila and Singapore had fallen – Isogai assumed office, dining at the Peninsula with Sakai and posing for photographers on the steps of the hotel in his military uniform and jackboots.

'I have humbly received the great responsibility of being Governor of the captured territory of Hong Kong, and today I have arrived in person to the place,' he proclaimed. 'As for those who transgress the path of right and do not keep within their right places, I will deal with these according to military law, without mercy.'

The day following his arrival, he landed on Hong Kong Island and toured it in a motorcade, stopping at Upper Albert Road for a while 'to inspect the residence of the former British Governor'.[1]

Isogai did not choose, like Young and his predecessors, to live and work at Government House. The building was cracking open and clearly unsafe; besides, it was not Japanese practice for military governors to have their residence and office under the same roof.

He set up the Governor's Office in the bank building where the civil administration was already established and in front of it erected his fearsome proclamation, in place of Queen Victoria's statue. Japanese practice notwithstanding, he lived for a short spell where he worked, commandeering the former bank chairman's flat on the ninth floor and riding the lift down to his office each morning at 10.

Then Isogai and his household moved, not out to quiet Fanling Lodge in the New Territories nor up to what remained of Mountain Lodge in its gardens of hydrangea but to an empty European villa overlooking the sea on the left of the road down to Repulse Bay.

For reasons of prestige, however, the new administration believed something should be done about Government House. Feltham, the expert on governors' residences, was brought in from Stanley camp

Isogai, 'Governor of the captured territory'

to the bank for questioning.

'Your Governor,' a Japanese official told him politely, 'must be a very brave man to have lived in a building in that condition.'

Isogai decided to rebuild on the same site.

Since he knew Manchuria and had a relative who was an architect with the South Manchurian Railway Company, he asked the company to take charge of the project. What was stipulated, says Kinya Nakao who was Isogai's senior adjutant, was a building that would symbolise Japan's military aspirations but that would also, when peace came, serve as civil governor's residence, place of work and VIP guest-house. The design had to blend the styles of the West and traditional Japan; and for economy's sake it had to retain as much as possible of the existing building.

On Major Nakao's recommendation, 26-year-old engineer Seichi Fujimura was sent down to prepare working drawings and see the job through.

'A sketch by an architect with the railroad company called Kensuke Aiga had already been approved,' says Fujimura today, 'and I took charge of the practical design. I would have liked to build a modern Government House but Isogai and the government officials wanted to incorporate traditional Japanese architecture.'

Bowing to authority, he sketched a series of more or less exotic variations on Aiga's basic theme. The drawings Isogai received were complete down to the figures of Japanese soldiers strolling on

Fujimura's flight of fancy: the north face

the north lawns past a magnolia tree beloved of successive British governors.[2]

Officialdom trimmed young Fujimura's wilder flights of fancy. None the less, within two years of Isogai's arrival, Government House (now standing not on Upper Albert Road facing the Botanical Gardens but on Nakataisho-dori facing the Taisho Koyen) was a tiered and turreted East/West hybrid vaguely reminiscent of Japanese palaces, the Imperial Hotel in Tokyo and even, from some aspects, Fanling Lodge – though Fujimura and Feltham never met.

Contrary to first appearances, Fujimura's Government House was not a totally new building. Being structurally sound, the ballroom annexe had been retained even to the ornamental bronze lamps of the roof-garden, Palmer and Turner's pillars and pediments simply being streamlined to suit Japanese taste. The dominant new central tower in fact stood over the old flight of steps from house to annexe, linking the two buildings more aesthetically than they had ever been linked. And although Cleverly's sagging mansion had been largely demolished and replaced by a smooth structure in reinforced concrete, his original ground-plan had been scrupulously retained.

No prewar occupant of Government House would have had any difficulty in finding his way around, at least at garden and ground level. Hall, dining-room, drawing-room, faun's-head conservatory, period-piece ballroom, supper-room, steps and staircases were precisely where they had been before, even if their function was not

Fujimura: the south face

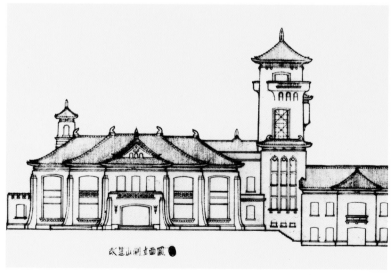

always the same; some stretches of 1850s balustrade and basement corridor survived; and so, because it too was sound, did Cleverly's pleasant gate-lodge.

The contractor for the job was the Formosan branch of Japan's Shimizu Construction, using local subcontractors who included Sang Lee.

Traditional Japanese roof pottery to top off the edifice, Fujimura obtained from Occupied China through the railway company. What arrived was unsatisfactory – the symbolic 'halberd' to go on the big tower, he says, was nothing like his specification – but it had to be used since a deadline had been set for completion.

A professional landscape gardener was brought down from Kyoto to work on the grounds; and a firm of interior decorators in Osaka handled furnishings.[3]

The focal point of the rebuilt hall was a life-size wooden *samurai* wearing a suit of armour dating from the Tokunawa era. To one side of it stood a stuffed tiger – the famous tiger shot on Stanley peninsula in 1942.

Both *samurai* and tiger served to foster the requisite fighting spirit but while the *samurai* was obtained at considerable trouble from Kyoto, the tiger arrived by chance, carried in by the Indians who had shot it. The staff at Government House, says Nakao, ate some of the meat 'out of curiosity' while the skin was sent to Tokyo to be stuffed as a trophy.

Upstairs, facing the harbour, a traditional Japanese *tatami* suite was created for the Governor, complete with raised floors and sliding screens. Isogai was a master of tea ceremony and Nakao added a small tea-ceremony room. Across the landing, facing the Peak, the Governor was provided with a Western-style bedroom.

Items taken from various deserted European homes were used to furnish those rooms that stayed Western-style, but the traffic was two-way. Dr P. S. Selwyn Clarke, Director of Medical Services under the British, was initially retained by the Japanese and to dinner with him and his wife Hilda on May Road one night came a Captain Yamaguchi, followed by a chauffeur carrying a large portfolio.

From this portfolio, having dined, Yamaguchi produced a complete 78 rpm recording of the Kreutzer Sonata and proceeded to play it all the way through on the toy, wind-up gramophone which was all that was available.

How had he managed to find such records, asked a guest.

'The captain, after lovingly putting his records away in the album, looked about for his sword. "I found them in Government House," he said absently, "the day after the surrender." He picked up his sword and buckled it on. He bowed low to us all, clicking his heels, and then went out into the dark, accompanied to the car by Selwyn with a lantern. "The Governor's records," said Hilda. "Sir Mark was very fond of Beethoven." '[4]

More usefully, long-term, one of the Chinese subcontractors working on the demolition of Cleverly's mansion in 1942 salvaged some pictures from the Chater collection.

'I first entered Government House about the middle of June,' stated Sinn Chi Lam, the subcontractor in question. 'The place was guarded by *Kempeitai,* Indian policemen and Japanese soldiers. Everything valuable had been removed. There were a few broken sofas and broken safes. On the walls I saw three large oil paintings of royal personages which had been slashed across and one which was intact. I persuaded a Japanese guard to let me have the good canvas, on the plea that I wanted it as a mattress cover and after paying him ¥50 and two packets of cigarettes. This bribe also covered packages which I made up of old prints recovered from the rubbish and broken glass littering the floor. I took the frames from these and smuggled a few out at suitable times.'[5]

Isogai to Tanaka

FOR the first couple of years, while Government House was being rebuilt, Isogai gave his formal indoor parties and receptions at the Peninsula, reopened as the 'Toa' hotel soon after his arrival. The Cricket Club ground opposite the Supreme Court, now 'the sports ground opposite the Gendarmerie Headquarters', he used for outdoor functions that might otherwise have been held in the grounds of Government House. Visiting Japanese VIPs paid their courtesy calls on him at the Governor's Office in the bank building.

On February 20, 1943, Isogai acknowledged the first anniversary of his governorship with a programme that embraced all three sites. At the Toa, he hosted a tiffin party that the *Hongkong News* described (reminiscently) as 'one of the most brilliant gatherings of the year'. On the sports ground, he and his officials bowed in the direction of Tokyo and the Imperial Palace. At the Governor's Office, he received representatives of the two Chinese councils that had replaced the executive and legislative councils. And at the Taisho Koyen, opposite what was left of the prewar Government House, he threw in for good measure a fireworks display.[6]

Five months later, 'Japanese ceremonial rites in connection with the building of the Governor's House at Nakataisho-dori were conducted before a large gathering of distinguished officials, including His Excellency the Governor'.[7]

Ceremony 'at the new Government House', February 1944

THE HONGKONG NEWS, MONDAY, FEBRUARY 21, 1944. Registered as third-class mai Showa 17th Year, Augu

THE
JGKONG
JEWS

ONGKONG
ead Office:
lakasumiyoshi-dori.
31243 and 31244.
& Business Offices:
Wyndham Street.
'elephones:
& Business Dept.—
6615-26617
sing Dept.—24444
s Dept.—26768
O ETO, PUBLISHER.
ble Address
)" HONGKONG.

uffle Of
abinet

g determination of
people and Govern-
rcome all obstacles in
final victory and thus
new order in East
n justice and righte-
affected in the partial
the Cabinet announc-
loard of Information

the nature of ordin-
measures and in line
langes in ministries
rs carried out last
ing the Diet session,
ell-informed political
kyo have pointed out,

Governor's Office Anniversary

Whole Community Extends Felicitations To Governor

High officials of the Governor's Office, Army and Navy Officers, and representatives of all sections of the community, including a number of women, gathered at the new Government House yesterday to offer their felicitations to His Excellency the Governor, Lieut-General Rensuke Isogai, on the occasion of the second anniversary of the establishment of the Governor's Office in Hongkong.

The gathering, which numbered nearly a thousand, assembled in the reception hall, and after respects had been paid to the Imperial Palace, during which the band played the Japanese National Anthem, "Kamigayo," and to the Ise Grand Shrine, one minute's silence was observed for the war dead as well as to strengthen the determination to prosecute the war to a successful conclusion, thus attaining the final object of establishing Greater East Asia.

His Excellency the Governor then addressed the gathering. He said in part:

"Today marks the second anniversary of the establishment of the Governor's Office, and amidst our joys and celebrations I wish to take this opportunity to express my thanks and gratitude to you all for your wholehearted co-operation during the two years of my administration.

"The necessity of applying

PHOTO above shows His Excellency the Governor exchanging a toast with the guests at a reception held in Government House

A

In or
have n
per pro
address
cided t
Februa
yesterd
not mi

The
day's s
of the
establis
Office,
will be
24. Re
four da
days of

Firev
for dis
all th
official
ties.

Since
of distr
public t
of mar
increas
ed the
this co
tion Sy
ther su
for sale
ing of
very sh

Peninsula Hotel, alias the 'Toa'

The reconstruction, having started, went through fast. Fujimura was working simultaneously on a massive war memorial at Mount Cameron but by 1944 his Government House was complete and Isogai was able to use it to celebrate the second anniversary of his governorship.

'High officials of the Governor's Office, army and navy officers, and representatives of all sections of the community, including a number of women,' reported the *Hongkong News* on February 21, 'gathered at the new Government House yesterday to offer their felicitations to His Excellency the Governor.

'The gathering, which numbered nearly a thousand, assembled in the reception hall and after respects had been paid to the Imperial Palace, during which the band played the Japanese national anthem "Kamigayo", and to the Ise Grand Shrine, one minute's silence was observed for the war dead, as well as to strengthen the determination to prosecute the war to a successful conclusion thus attaining the final object of establishing Greater East Asia . . .

'The gathering was honoured with *sake* graciously presented by His Imperial Majesty the Emperor of Japan to His Excellency the Governor. The wine was specially brought to Hong Kong by an Imperial Messenger.'

Isogai in Hong Kong, performing the tea ceremony

Two months later, on April 29, the Emperor's birthday was celebrated at Government House, with bows towards Tokyo and a pledge to redouble the war effort.

Neither celebration was elaborate and no attention was drawn to the splendours of the new house. The war was turning against Japan. On mainland Asia Japanese forces were still advancing but in the Pacific they had been checked. Hong Kong as a whole was in a sorry shape, its population more than halved by forcible repatriation to Kwangtung, with rice and fuel in chronically short supply. It was no time for parties.

'The war has entered the decisive stage,' Isogai told his guests on that second anniversary, 'and possibly we may have to suffer more and more.' In the circumstances, he said, he had decided to celebrate the occasion in a very simple manner and give a day's free supply of rice to Hong Kong residents in lieu.

The Governor was not in any case living extravagantly. Even when Fujimura's Government House was finished, he did not move into it, finding Repulse Bay both more congenial and more economical.

Whatever the Japanese military record in Hong Kong over all, Isogai himself was not the terror his proclamation and jackboots suggested. Retired from active service by the time Japan declared war, he was glad to be well behind the front line. In the 1930s he had tried to stop Japan's war with China and he saw himself as a protector of the Chinese in Hong Kong. He had a reputation for good living and geisha parties that, according to Nakao, was unwarranted. Isogai, Nakao says, liked the simple life and much preferred to be studying calligraphy in his house near the sea and walking out into its garden in his slippers to listen to the croaking of the bullfrogs. One of the few times he used Government House in his private capacity was to perform the tea ceremony.

Such days were almost over, however. Island by island, the Pacific was being retaken by the Allies. Conditions were difficult, admitted the 60-year-old Isogai to the press in December 1944, and likely to become even more difficult.

The following month, as Japan began preparing for the worst, he was replaced by a man still in active service – the Commander of the 23rd Japanese Arm and the C-in-C South China, Lt-General Hisakazu Tanaka.

Isogai returned to Japan to report to the Emperor. Arriving from Canton, the new Governor of Hong Kong attended a ceremony at what had been St John's Cathedral, in memory of those killed in an American air-raid that hit Stanley camp.

In February, the Americans re-entered Manila. On April 29, Hong Kong celebrated the Emperor's birthday for the last time.

A week later, Germany surrendered. On August 15, so did Japan. Tanaka issued an official statement giving Hong Kong the news but appealing to the public to 'remain calm and continue to work as usual'. Japan's occupation was over.

11 Reoccupation

(1945-46)

INTERNEES began leaving Stanley almost immediately. Two of the first out were Colonial Secretary Gimson and John Deakin who had been official Government House 'custodian' before the war. Both men headed for town.

Gimson managed to contact London and was told to take over as Lieutenant-Governor pending the arrival of a military administration. This he did, setting up his headquarters in the French Mission[1] at the top of Battery Path – on the site, as it happened, of the 1840s Government House that belonged to A. R. Johnston.

Deakin, detailed by Gimson to help get Government House in shape, made for the old building he had known, keen to look for his possessions and a bottle of brandy he had hidden there in December 1941, before Hong Kong fell.

'The Japanese had already fled the place,' said an Australian fellow-internee who went along, making no reference to its metamorphosis, 'so it was deserted and very eerie. Deacon (*sic*) dug by a tree in the garden and retrieved the brandy, four years older and all the better for it. While he scrounged around for a few other things, I nicked a couple of Japanese ashtrays. which I still have. Then Deacon said, "Let's go back to the Mission and have ourselves a celebration."

'It was a celebration to remember . . . It was simply glorious. We had tongue, biscuits and butter – real butter – and all sorts of other things which he had hidden in Government House before going into camp. We ate the lot. All by ourselves.'[2]

On August 30, Rear Admiral Cecil Harcourt sailed into the harbour at the head of a British task force, to take the surrender and administer the colony.

'By nightfall of the first day,' reported the *South China Morning Post*, 'the city of Victoria had unmistakably been taken over by the navy. The Gloucester Hotel almost blazed with lights from the suites taken over by His Excellency the Governor and his staff, and other naval personnel.'

On September 5, Harcourt and his aides moved to Upper Albert Road.

'The old Government House, rebuilt by the Japanese and constructed in an entirely different and oriental style, has been cleaned out,' said the *Post*. 'Any major reconstruction will be done later.'

The following day, an open letter to the colony was published, written by Sir Mark Young in Chungking. He had been in prison camps in Shanghai, Formosa and Manchuria, and had seen no one from Hong Kong for the first three years.

Young returned to England to recuperate, as did Gimson. David MacDougall, a government official who had escaped from Hong Kong on Christmas Day 1941, came back as Chief Civil Affairs

Surrender ceremony at Government House. Harcourt (top) and Fujita (below)

Officer with powers of the Governor-in-council although Harcourt stayed on at Government House as Commander-in-Chief.

And on September 16, at the house they had rebuilt, the Japanese officially surrendered Hong Kong in a short, severe ceremony.

Vice-Admiral Ruitako Fujita, Commander of the South China Fleet, and Major-General Umekichi Okada, local garrison commander, were brought across from Whitfield Barracks. Guarded by commandos with tommy-guns, they stood in the main hall behind a small table bearing brushes and an ink slab. Harcourt and official military observers from China, the United States and Canada sat opposite, at a larger table. Harcourt read out the Instrument of Surrender and the Japanese officers affixed their chops, 'given under our hands this 16th day of September, 1945, at Government House, Hong Kong'. Then they handed over their swords.

'Neither Japanese,' commented the *China Mail*, 'uttered a single word throughout the proceedings. They did as they were bid, stood at attention while Admiral Harcourt appended his signature in witness, bowed stiffly from the waist and were then marched away.

'An able seaman very slowly hoisted the Union Jack.'

'It was a scene etched against the background of a magnificently rejuvenated Government House, which gave the Japanese no opportunity of evading the humiliation of their position, and it was perhaps apt that the ceremony should have taken place in the only building which, judging by the spacious grandeur of its interior, had furnished their high ranking officers with moments of pride in achievement.'

When Fujita and Okada had gone, back to the barracks as prisoners of war, 'came the most impressive part of all,' said the BBC in an emotional broadcast from Hong Kong that night. 'The Royal Marine band struck up the national anthem and, as it was being played, an able seaman very slowly hoisted the Union Jack on the flagstaff opposite the gate. And then pandemonium broke loose in the harbour as every warship thundered out a 21-gun salute . . . the roars echoed and re-echoed from the face of the Peak . . . Corsairs of the Fleet Air Arm roared overhead at almost housetop level.'

Two out of three

AFTER the celebrations came the sorting out. To those who had not seen it since 1941, Hong Kong looked a mess. Virtually no maintenance had been done on harbour, roads or installations. Catchwaters and storm drains were blocked by landslides and rubbish. Most of the trees had been cut down for timber but the Peak, scarcely used, was a tangle of undergrowth. Unguarded buildings had been stripped to the walls. Even public statues were missing from their pedestals.

In 3½ years, the Japanese had built only two things of any significance – Fujimura's huge skyline memorial on Mount Cameron and his Government House. The former was dynamited; the latter was retained. Harcourt, the story goes, received instructions from London to reconstruct what in 1941 had been a tottering Governor's residence. 'Not necessary,' he is supposed to have replied, looking at the prewar plans for a house at Magazine Gap. 'The Japanese have done the job for us.'

What was necessary, however, was new furnishings. There was no trace, for instance, of silver Sir Mark Young had had to leave behind nor of the Chater collection pictures; and some of the larger items at the house were being narrowly eyed by returning residents.

'Dear Sir,' wrote Albert Raymond of Sassoon Banking to Harcourt's ADC on September 21, 1945. 'During the Japanese occupation of Hong Kong, the Japanese governor and his staff resided in my house and my brother's house next door in Nos 41 and 43 Repulse Bay Road. I understand that when they shifted to Government House they took all our furniture with them.

'This is to ask His Excellency Admiral Harcourt's permission for me and my wife to go to Government House in order to identify any such furniture. Incidentally the above two houses are in perfect condition but bare of any furniture.'

Standard Vacuum Oil had a similar story of requisitioned furniture and subsequently identified two dozen chairs and a bed at Government House as coming from the company residence on Barker Road.

It had been decided that Young would resume his governorship in April 1946 and in January, from England, he asked for a brief account of the state of Government House furnishings and of what might need to be shipped out.

The request overlapped with the arrival in Hong Kong of Admiral Lord Louis Mountbatten, Supreme Allied Commander South-East Asia, paying his first visit since 1922 when he had been the Prince of Wales' equerry and Government House was a thing of gracious European colonnades and terraces, with polo ponies stabled in the

Mountbatten. His first visit since 1922

Return to civil government. Young takes over.

grounds. The Government House that Harcourt showed him looked Japanese and most of its aesthetic touches were Japanese.

Back went a telegraph for Young. 'Following required: *a*) complete cutlery crockery crystal napery silver and kitchen utensils *b*) bedlinen, blankets *c*) covers for minimum five bedrooms *d*) curtains for 60 windows 12 by 5 feet. Suggest flowered cretonnes old rose predominating for bedrooms and dining room, old gold for lounge *e*) loose covers for 50 straight backed dining room chairs flowered cretonnes and for 15 upholstered chairs for lounge matching curtains *f*) pictures and ornaments etc completely lacking'.[3]

Young flew into Kai Tak on April 30 and was taken by Harcourt to a Government House he would not at first have recognised.

The following day, both men attended a ceremony in the main hall to mark the end of the military administration and a return to civil government. Sitting with them, behind the table at which Harcourt had received the Japanese surrender, 83-year-old Sir Robert Ho Tung read the returning Governor an address of welcome in Cantonese. It was the first time Young and Hong Kong's Grand Old Man had been at a function together since the Ho Tung diamond wedding festivities on December 2, 1941, six days before the Japanese attack.

Young, reinstated, initiated surveys of all three residences that governors of Hong Kong had enjoyed before the war. So many of the colony's European buildings had been destroyed or stripped that accommodation was desperately short, and he asked if Mountain Lodge could be made fit 'for occupation as a government quarter by two or more officials'. If it could, he would hand it over for a limited period.

But the lodge was past it.

'The brick walls are built with red earth joints which are disintegrating owing to their exposure to the elements for the last few years,' reported the PWD, 'and much of the woodwork has been attacked by white ants and would have to be stripped. Mountain Lodge would therefore have to be practically rebuilt.

'It was realised some years before the war that this house had passed its economic life. Maintenance costs were very heavy. Heating plant had to be installed to nurse the old damp walls and fittings, and the site was riddled with white ants. The lay-out was old-fashioned and out of date. It was not a comfortable house to live in and as a result was inhabited for only a very short period each year. Furthermore it was accessible only by the use of a small car.

'It is felt that the rehabilitation of Mountain Lodge would be perpetuating an out of date, uncomfortable and expensive house.'

Young accepted the advice and the lodge was demolished, leaving only its granite foundations, little gate-lodge and some mosaic tiling.[4] For the first time since 1867, the Governor of Hong Kong had no residence on the Peak.

Nor, in Young's opinion, did he need one. In August 1946, he announced that the Magazine Gap site still being reserved for a new Government House would not be so required. 'I agree,' he said, 'to its being earmarked for government quarters.'[5]

The surviving gate-lodge to Mountain Lodge

Fanling Lodge was in relatively good condition. All its doors had disappeared and some Japanese baths and outhouses would have to be removed but $16,000 would make the place habitable. Young announced that he did not want the lodge as a country residence during his tenure and assigned it to the Rural Teachers' Training College, which moved in in September 1946.[6]

At Government House itself, the furnishings were not yet right. Crystal and old-rose cretonne were hard to come by in immediately postwar Britain: the goods ordered by telegraph in February could not be shipped until August. And the Japanese suite still occupied the best part of the upper floor.

'It was a beautiful suite of four or five rooms,' recalls ex-internee Michael Wright, who later became Director of Public Works. 'Formosan pine, most beautiful work, was used for the rice-paper sliding screens. They were complete Japanese rooms with bathrooms attached, bathrooms with square marble seats where you could sit and have the servant throw water over you. But Sir Mark Young hated them and ordered us to get rid of them.'

Plans were prepared by Feltham (back in harness) for the removal of the offending screens, doors and raised floors; and for the construction in their place of four 'proper' bedrooms with new bathrooms. Sang Lee won the contract and started pulling out the fittings they may have helped to put in.

By Christmas 1946, with the jettisoning of the *tatami* and the arrival of the old rose, the interior of Government House was British again.[7]

12 Since 1946

Sir Mark Young stayed only a year, during the whole of which (although Isogai and Tanaka were tried in China) Japanese war crimes trials were conducted in Hong Kong.

Shortly before he left, the Governor presented awards to some of Hong Kong's heroes in the war against Japan, including those villages and villagers responsible for helping Allied prisoners escape into Free China. Sai Kung, Sha Tin, Sha Tau Kok, Tai Po, Lantau, Cheung Chau, and Shau Kei Wan and Joss House Bay were singled out. Families, clansmen and district elders, 180 in all, packed in to watch. It was one of the largest insignia presentation ceremonies ever held at Government House, and perhaps the most popular.[1]

Treasure-hunt

The search for the Chater collection was meanwhile beginning to read like a first-class mystery. The porcelain, which had been in Government Stores at North Point, had disappeared without trace, believed shipped straight to Japan. Items were turning up, though, from the picture collection. Sinn Chi Lam brought back from his country home in China the 20 or so prints (and portrait of Queen Mary) he had salvaged from the old Government House and returned them to the government at the end of 1946. Portuguese resident F. A. Xavier donated 30 pictures he had recovered from shops around the colony. In 1948, three oils were discovered in the vaults of the Hongkong and Shanghai Bank. Nineteen maps and prints surfaced at Hong Kong University.

Altogether, by the summer of 1950, some 75 of the 400 pictures were back in government hands. By and large, however, they were among the least valuable items of the whole collection. None of the Chinnery originals had come to light.

'The Japanese are going to rebuild Government House and they are getting So-and-so of the PWD out of Stanley to advise them about the foundations, especially that air-raid shelter,' the Hungarian Von Kobza Nagy had told the editor of the *South China Morning Post* during the occupation. 'I'm afraid they'll find the secret chamber. We hid there the best of the Chater collection.'[2] And to an Austrian friend he had said that the pictures had been cut out of their frames, put into specially prepared metal tubes, sealed and buried hastily at the last minute.

But Von Kobza, Batty-Smith and Harmon had all died, taking with them any knowledge of the exact hiding-place.

The Hungarian's chief assistant, Fung Ming, said in 1945 that he knew his employer had been called in to discuss the safe-keeping of the paintings. 'I do not know where these paintings were stored. Mr Kobza did tell me it was a secret and he was on his honour to keep the secret for the government.'

Claude Burgess, working under MacDougall as head of the secretariat and hearing the various stories, became convinced that Von Kobza – whom he had known – would have buried the paintings in the grounds of Government House at dead of night. He said so to Admiral Harcourt.

'He was greatly interested, partly I think because stories of buried treasure always appeal to sailors and partly because the idea of restoring anything to Hong Kong, which he loved, was sure to fire his enthusiasm. "All right," he said, "let's dig. But I want it done professionally. You should get the PWD to put some special chaps on to it, and please tell them to make as little mess as possible."

'I duly did this . . . Two or three months passed and there was still no result. One day I was at a Government House meeting and the Admiral finished off the business and then turned and contemplated me with a jaundiced eye that was not without a twinkle. "Burgess," he growled, "get out of my garden. God knows, I've got little enough time to enjoy this glorious job and I demand that I have at least a month or two to enjoy my garden." I conveyed his instructions to the PWD and that was the end.'

Sir Mark Young, when he took over, was evidently unable to throw any new light on the subject; and Harmon, said his wife, had never mentioned it.

Then in September 1950 a letter arrived from Deakin, the ex-custodian of Government House, in reply to a suggestion by Austin Coates of the Secretariat that some Chater collection pictures might have been buried in the garden. It was news to him, wrote Deakin the hider of brandy, that any pictures were thought to have been hidden in the grounds.

'Before any of the collection was hid (that is, that part which was at Government House), some of the collection was sent down to be stored in the Inspector of Furniture's store at Wan Chai. The balance as far as I was concerned was hid in the strong room, wine cellar and crockery stores which were then situated in the basement underneath Government House. Some of the most valuable personal effects of Sir Mark Young were also hid in these stores, also Captain Batty-Smith's personal effects and my own household things.

'On being released from Stanley camp I was detailed by Mr Gimson to report to Government House to help get Government House staffed and put in fit state for Admiral Harcourt and his staff to occupy. On my arrival at Government House, I can assure you, my first visit was to the basement where I found that all the old basement stores had been demolished and new ones built and there was no sign of any of the Chater collection or our personal property.'

The drawing-room today. Chandeliers but no Chater collection

That was enough for Coates, who was organising an exhibition of the surviving pictures. In a radio talk, he summarised the position as he saw it:

'Shortly before the Japanese attack, Sir Mark Young ordered that all the more valuable pictures, including the Chinnerys, should be stored in the strong room and wine cellar underneath Government House. A few remaining lithographs stayed in their places on the walls of the Governor's residence.

'Then, two days before the Japanese reached Hong Kong territory, the Governor's ADC sent for two people, one a Hungarian artist who had formerly assisted in restoring and maintaining the Chater collection, the other an officer of the PWD. No one knows exactly what happened at that interview but . . . it has been ascertained that the two men were entrusted with secreting the Chater pictures . . .

'At the end of the war the official who had put the pictures in the wine cellar and knew nothing about the subsequent interview with the Governor's ADC, went in search of them only to discover that in the course of the alterations effected to the house by the Japanese, the cellars had been destroyed and rebuilt entirely. If therefore, as seems likely, the hiding-place was somewhere in the wall or floor of one of the cellars, it is almost certain that during the renovations the Japanese discovered it and took the pictures away to Japan.'

At this stage, the *Tiger Standard* tracked down Sinn Chi Lam who now volunteered that it was in the wine cellar and adjoining strong room that he had accidentally found his 20 prints, in May 1942. On October 16, 1950, the paper printed a photograph of him taken in 1942 among the basement rubble of Government House 'near the entrance of the air-raid tunnel in which he once hid these pictures' and it quoted him as saying that any other pictures must already have been stolen by the time he got there.

Two months later, in Tokyo, an oil painting of a British warship that had turned up 'among sundry items which the Japanese stated had been looted from unknown areas', was identified as belonging to the Chater collection.[3]

Since then a couple more prints have been handed in. The Chinnerys are still missing although, sporadically, the hunt for them is revived. In 1976, the grounds of Government House were scanned with sophisticated army equipment. Some rusty old piping was all that showed up.

To keep or not to keep

YOUNG had only converted the Japanese suite. Sir Alexander Grantham, who succeeded him and stayed to become Hong Kong's longest-serving Governor to date, elected to overhaul the entire house. Or, rather, his wife Maurine did.

The Granthams arrived in July 1947 and within a month so many alterations were in hand that PWD had an Inspector of Works at Upper Albert Road on virtually full-time duty. False ceilings and cantilevered balconies; air-conditioning and rewiring; new fireplaces, panelling, chandeliers; extensions, decorations; floodlighting and two sculptured lions to greet the Duchess of Kent . . .

Guests streamed in, from Nehru and Field Marshal Slim to Elizabeth Taylor and Mike Todd; attendance at garden-parties hit 4,500; and the more visitors that arrived, the more improvements to the facilities were found to be necessary.

'By the time she had finished,' Grantham wrote later of his wife, 'Government House was something of which people of Hong Kong were proud.'[4]

Yet he thought a different house was needed. In September 1947 the new Governor reversed Young's decision to release Magazine Gap, effectively sterilising the site for yet another decade.

Hong Kong's population was now back to its prewar strength of 1.6 million, and still rising. In China, the renewed civil war between nationalists and communists was reaching a climax. On October 1, 1949, Mao Tse-tung proclaimed the People's Republic. The communists took Canton and their troops appeared on the border.

Cleverly's gate-lodge and Fujimura's tower

Within 12 months, refugees had swollen Hong Kong's population to 2.3 million. In 1956, it was over 2.5 million.

When the legislative council debated that March the urgent shortage of land in the city and unofficial Dhun Ruttonjee suggested selling 'dusty old edifices' like the GPO on Pedder Street and getting rid of Government House at the same time, Grantham went along with him. The public rooms of the house were inadequate, he told the council, for a colony getting so many visitors and such a large population. A new Government House was needed.

'Happily,' he said, 'there is a suitable site available: that is, the site at Magazine Gap which was earmarked for this purpose more than 25 years ago.

'The question also arises, "What to do with the present Government House?" I imagine that it would be extremely difficult to convert for any other purpose. What then to do with the site? . . . I am assured by leading hotel authorities that the ideal site for a first-class hotel on the island is Government House. I leave these thoughts to honourable members.'[5]

Honourable members dropped the subject but the press stepped in to deplore – albeit politely – any notion that Government House should be moved to the Peak.

'There is much to be said,' intoned the *South China Morning Post* in an editorial straight out of the 19th century, 'for close contact between a Governor and his population: an impressive Government House, constantly and closely in view, presents the vice-regal majesty and contributes appreciably to a colony's political atmosphere . . . there will doubtless be many residents urging that the new Government House should occupy the site of the old one – especially if there is to be no Governor's Office close to the city.' Still, the writer trailed off, if the site *had* to be sold to a hotel company, let it be sold for its full market value.[6]

The Nineties ballroom, with coat of arms from Peking

The *China Mail* thought Government House was 'in the right place' where it was. If it had to go, however, let the site be turned into a park. 'And why not,' asked the *Mail*, 'incorporate some of the features of English municipal gardens: provision of a tea-house, an open-air swimming pool, a miniature golf course and putting green? From these amenities would be derived revenue sufficient to pay for the upkeep of the place.'[7]

Grantham did not press his suggestion further. He left Hong Kong the following year; and in 1958 Sir Robert Black, his successor, released the Magazine Gap site,[8] saying he believed Government House should stay where it was.

'I considered it important,' he explains today, 'to keep the Governor's residence where it had long stood, where it was patently in the midst of Hong Kong's day-to-day life and where the Governor was obviously looking at it all and not away from it all. In the inevitable absence of representative government, in the ordinary and familiar sense, I did not wish to be, far less appear to be, remote.'

Two years later, in 1960, Black retrieved Fanling Lodge from the military to whom the Granthams had passed it over. The country house near the border with China, for which there had originally been such hopes as a seat of goodwill, had been out of action as a Governor's residence for nearly 20 of its 25 years.

Black's town and country decisions have so far been upheld. In the 1960s, under Sir David Trench, Government House received a further $1.5 million overhaul that ensured its retention in its present form for at least another decade or two. In the course of it, part of the one-room-per-storey Japanese tower was converted into quarters for the housekeeper, giving her the most spectacularly inconvenient eyrie in Hong Kong. Sixty feet below, the Nineties ballroom had already acquired a Nineties coat of arms presented during Black's governorship by the British Legation in Peking.

In May 1967, during China's Cultural Revolution, the house unexpectedly made world headlines when, for several days in succession, communist agitators plastered Cleverly's old gate-lodge with seditious posters and, refused permission to petition the Governor in a body, stood outside the walls chanting slogans from *The thoughts of Mao*.

The following March, righting the balance, Trench threw Government House grounds open to the public, allowing anyone who wished to wander through and see the azaleas that now blazed away each spring on the banks facing the harbour.

Azalea Day at Government House has since become an institution drawing 100,000 people – more than the total population of the colony when house and grounds were first laid out.

The house continues to double as home and place of work as it has for each British governor since Bowring moved into it in 1855, although the emphasis has progressively shifted away from private residence to official-functions centre.

Luxuries like billiard-room and conservatory have been cut out in favour of more office space. Presentation ceremonies are held more often than balls and banquets. Meet-the-people lunches, dinners and receptions have superseded the old 'establishment' socialising to the extent that every year more than 7,500 residents are invited. At the same time, the list of house-guests has lengthened to include many heads of state and most working members of the British royal family.

In May 1975, Queen Elizabeth II became Britain's first reigning monarch to visit Hong Kong. As the guests of Governor Sir Murray MacLehose, she and Prince Philip drove through Cleverly's old gate-lodge to stay in a Government House which, for all its exotic additions and for all Hong Kong's propensity to change, still stands precisely where the first Governor, Pottinger, planned that it should, early in the reign of the Queen's great-great-grandmother. Upper Albert Road has now been the residence of Hong Kong's governors for over 120 years.

Notes

Official records referred to below are held as follows:
Series HKMS 36, HKMS 40, HKRS 149, HKRS 170, HKRS 193 – Public
Records Office, Hong Kong
Buildings and Lands Branch correspondence files (BL, etc.) – Environment
Branch, Secretariat, Hong Kong
Correspondence file (GR, etc.) and prints – Hong Kong Museum of Art
Government House plans (20th century) – Architectural Office, PWD, Hong
Kong
Colonial Office records including Government House/Mountain Lodge plans
(19th century), Series CO 129 – Public Record Office, London
Foreign Office records, Series FO 925 – Public Record Office, London

1 Record Office on Government Hill (1841–44)

[1] *Chinese Repository,* Vol X, referring to 21/22 August 1841. Granville Loch,
referring to the same occasion, writes in *The closing events of the campaign
in China* (John Murray, London, 1843): 'when Sir Henry Pottinger first
landed, he lived in a pitched tent!'

[2] *Canton Press,* 15 January 1842. An 1842 map, 'Pottinger's West' (FO 925/2427),
has a building on Government Hill marked 'Record Office Present Government
House'. Subsequent maps and references show that this stood on the site
of the covered reservoir opposite the main entrance to today's Government
House, e.g. in May 1843 an estimate was passed for 'a treasury opposite
Government House' (i.e. opposite the Record Office) and in 1848 the treasury
was pulled down 'for the preparation of the site for Government House'
(i.e. today's site). The Record Office site was identified by Dafydd Evans in
Hong Kong's first Government House, Hong Kong Royal Asiatic Society
paper, 1968.

[3] 'For Superintendent's Office, Record Office and a house for two clerks:
$7,565.41', Pottinger to A. R. Johnston, 26 May 1842, Vol 10, CO 129.
A register of marriages (St John's Cathedral records, HKMS 40, D&S 1/13)
shows that 22 weddings were held 'in the Government House at Hong Kong'
from 1842–43.

[4] Richard Woosnam to A. T. Gordon, 18 April 1843, Vol 10, CO 129

[5] *Friend of China,* 1 June 1843

[6] Pottinger to A. R. Johnston, 21 October 1843, Vol 10, CO 129. Johnston's
house was on Inland Lot 82, the site of today's Victoria District Court at the
top of Battery Path. Pottinger had tendered his resignation by this time and
it is not clear whether he moved into the house himself or whether it was
used initially as offices. A drawing by E. Ashworth of what seems to be
Johnston's house is reproduced in *The Chater collection* (see chapter 9, note[1]),
captioned 'Sir H. Pottinger's house. 1845'. (It is reproduced here on page 7.)
Pottinger left Hong Kong in 1844, however, and in 1845 Governor David was
living in Johnston's house (see chapter 2). Hong Kong's first governors may of
course have lived at a number of unrecorded addresses.

[7] A. T. Gordon to G. A. Malcolm, 6 July 1843, Vol 2, CO 129

[8] Pottinger/D'Aguilar correspondence, January/February 1844, Vols 5/10,
CO 129

[9] Pottinger to Lord Stanley, 14 February 1844, and Stanley's reply of 4 June
1844, Vol 5, CO 129. In May 1845, the Spanish/Mexican dollar in use was
fixed at 4s2d.

2 Johnston's house to Caine's house (1844–48)

[1] Davis to Lord Stanley, 17 June 1844, Vol 6, CO 129

[2] Davis to Lord Stanley, 16 August 1844, Vol 7, CO 129

[3] List of government buildings as at 1 May 1845, Vol 12, CO 129

[4] Davis to Lord Stanley, 26 July 1845, Vol 12, CO 129

[5] Davis to Lord Stanley, 24 October 1845, Vol 13, CO 129

[6] Davis to Lord Stanley, 24 February 1846, Vol 16, CO 129. The 'newly erected
barracks' included today's Murray House. 'Government Offices' here = the
Record Office complex.

[7] Caine's house, built in 1845, was on Inland Lot 59 on what was already

'Caine's Road'. A one-year lease was drawn up between Caine and Davis on 2 February 1846 (HKRS 149, D&S 2/27).

[8] *Friend of China,* 18 April 1846

[9] See Bruce/Maclure lithograph, 'The residence of Lieut. Governor the Hon. Major General D'Aguilar, 28th September 1846'. Flagstaff House is due to be handed over to the government in March 1979 when Victoria Barracks is vacated by the British forces.

3 Caine's house to Spring Gardens (1848–50)

[1] Bonham to Earl Grey, 8 April 1848, Vol 24, CO 129. Bonham renewed the lease on Caine's house on 11 April 1848 at the same monthly rental of $250 (HKRS 149, D&S 2/87). The house hired for his servants was a bungalow opposite Caine's house, on Lot 141 (Cleverly, 9 February 1849, Vol 28, CO 129).

[2] Bonham to Earl Grey, 22 May 1848, Vol 24, CO 129

[3] Cleverly to Caine, 23 May 1848, Vol 24, CO 129

[4] Agreement between Caine and Assen, 3 July 1848, HKRS 149, D&S 2/82

[5] Bonham to Earl Grey, 1 September 1848, enclosing Caine/Cleverly/d'Almada Castro report dated 29 March 1848, Vol 26, CO 129

[6] *Tea-districts of China and India,* Robert Fortune. John Murray, London, 1852. In Bruce's drawing, 'View of Spring Gardens, 20th August 1846' (see Bruce/Maclure lithograph), the house is the second from the right. The site today, occupied by small shops, is bounded to north and south by Johnston Road (then under the sea) and Queen's Road East, between Lee Tung Street and Amoy Street.

[7] *Friend of China,* 23 June 1849. According to the relevant Blue Book, the rent was £625.

[8] *Friend of China,* 22 August 1849. The purchased court house was not Johnston's house (which the government finally gave up in February 1848) but a building on Marine Lots 7 and 61 further west along Queen's Road. The new Government Offices were approximately on the site of today's Central Government Offices on Lower Albert Road. The C-in-C's house was Head Quarter House, i.e. Flagstaff House (see chapter 2).

[9] Bonham to Earl Grey, 25 August 1849, Vol 30, CO 129

[10] Bonham to Earl Grey, 25 September 1850, Vol 34; Dent & Co. to Bonham, 13 March 1850, Vol 35, CO 129. C. J. Braine of Dent's lived at Green Bank, which was on Inland Lot 51 between Wyndham Street and Wellington Street.

4 The house Cleverly built (1851–58)

[1] The house Turner & Co. leased to the Governor (HKRS 149, D&S 2/116) stood on Marine Lot 43. In Bruce's drawing of Spring Gardens (see chapter 3), the house is third from the right. The Blue Books quote '£625 for rent of house occupied as Government House' from 1846 until completion of the house on Upper Albert Road.

[2] Government House plans (19th century). Cleverly's plans accompanied Bonham's despatch of 22 May 1848, Vol 24, CO 129.

[3] Cleverly, 12/14 February 1853, Blue Book for 1852

[4] Bonham to Duke of Newcastle, 22 September 1853, Vol 43, CO 129

[5] Bowring to Duke of Newcastle, 24 December 1853, Vol 44, CO 129

[6] Cleverly, 27 March 1854, Blue Book for 1853

[7] Cleverly, 28 March 1855, Blue Book for 1854

[8] Bowring to Lord John Russell, 4 September 1855, Vol 51, CO 129

[9] Cleverly, 7/11 February 1856, Blue Book for 1855. Cleverly mentions 'the new proprietors' of 'the premises tenanted by His Excellency'. Marine Lot 43 changed hands in 1855 – and again in 1856 ,HKRS 193, D&S 20/1), when it was advertised in the *Friend of China* of 20 September, e.g., as 'Old Government House'.

[10] Acting Surveyor General, T. L. Walker, 14 March 1857, Blue Book for 1856

[11] *The opening of Japan. A diary of discovery in the Far East 1853–56,* Rear-Admiral George Henry Preble. University of Oklahoma Press, 1902

[12] Bowring to H. Labouchère, 5 May 1856, Vol 55, CO 129

¹³ Bowring to Labouchère, 3 June 1856, Vol 56, CO 129
¹⁴ *To China and back, being a diary kept out and home,* Albert Smith. Published privately by the author, London, 1859; by Hong Kong University Press, 1974

5 Path to the Peak (1859–68)
¹ Robinson to Duke of Newcastle, 17 May 1860, Vol 77, CO 129
² Robinson to Duke of Newcastle, 10 January 1860, Vol 77, CO 129
³ Register of baptisms, St John's Cathedral records, HKMS 36, D&S 1/1
⁴ *Incidents in the China War of 1860 compiled from the private journals of General Sir Hope Grant,* Henry Knollys. William Blackwood & Sons, Edinburgh and London, 1875
⁵ Dr William Morrison, 21 February 1849, Blue Book for 1848
⁶ MacDonnell to Earl of Carnarvon, 30 January 1867, Vol 120, CO 129
⁷ MacDonnell to Duke of Buckingham, 24 March 1868, Vol 129, CO 129
⁸ MacDonnell to E. Cardwell, 11 May 1866, Vol 113, CO 129

6 The social round (1869–82)
¹ *Visit of His Royal Highness the Duke of Edinburgh,* Rev. William Beach. Noronha & Co., Hong Kong, 1869
² Kennedy to Earl of Kimberley, 29 October 1873, Vol 165, CO 129
³ *Hong Kong Daily Press,* 24 September 1874
⁴ *Hong Kong Daily Press,* 2 October 1874
⁵ Administrative Report for 1879
⁶ Hennessy/Donovan correspondence, May 1880, Vol 188, CO 129
⁷ Hennessy/Keswick correspondence, April-June 1881, Vol 193, CO 129
⁸ Hennessy/Hayllar correspondence, July 1881-February 1882, Vols 193/197, CO 129; *The Ananias Papers, containing correspondence relating to a dispute between the Hon. F. B. Johnson and the Rev. E. J. Eitel, 1882.* Published privately, Hong Kong
⁹ *China Mail,* 21 December 1881
¹⁰ *The cruise of HMS Bacchante, 1879–1882. Compiled from the private journals, letters and note-books of Prince Albert Victor and Prince George of Wales with additions by John N. Dalton.* Macmillan & Co., London, 1886

7 Private architecture (1883–1902)
¹ *My colonial service in British Guiana,* etc., Sir William Des Voeux, John Murray, London, 1903
² Samuel Brown, 10 July 1890, Sessional Papers for 1890
³ F. A. Cooper, 13 January 1892, Sessional Papers for 1891
⁴ Craigieburn was on Rural Building Lot 5, site of today's 'Hillcrest' apartment block facing the Peak School. It reverted to hotel in 1898.
⁵ Sir William Robinson to Marquis of Ripon, 17 November 1892, Vol 256, CO 129
⁶ HK Hansard for 17 July 1893. The Belilios property adjoining Mountain Lodge was 'The Eyrie' on Farm Lot 57. There is no residence there today.
⁷ The Cliffs was on Rural Building Lot 27, owned since 1903 by The Hongkong and Shanghai Banking Corporation which now has three 'Cliff' houses on the site.
⁸ HK Hansard for 13 March 1899
⁹ Blake to Joseph Chamberlain, 10 October 1899, Vol 294, CO 129
¹⁰ Sessional Papers 1901 (for 1900) and 1903 (for 1902); Blue Book for 1902; Mountain Lodge plans. The plans accompanied Blake's despatch of 10 October 1899 (see note ⁹).

8 Change of role (1903–25)
¹ *China Mail,* 20 November 1889
² HK Hansard for 28 March 1904
³ Nathan's papers, Rhodes House Library, Oxford
⁴ Lugard's papers, Rhodes House Library, Oxford; 'ample space for . . . quadrilles', *Twentieth century impressions of Hong Kong, Shanghai and other Treaty Ports.* London, 1908
⁵ *South China Morning Post,* 28 September 1909; *Hongkong Telegraph,* 27/28 September 1909

[6] 'E.G.S.' in *The Volunteer,* Journal of the Royal Hong Kong Defence Corps, 1854–1954 centenary number

9 Town and country (1926–41)
[1] 'Chater collection' file, GR 1/3371/46; *The Chater collection. Pictures relating to China, Hong Kong, Macao, 1655–1860,* James Orange. Thornton Butterworth Ltd, London, 1924
[2] Administrative Report for 1929; Government House plans
[3] HK Hansard for 6 October 1932
[4] Rural Building Lot 140. The sanatorium, erected in 1883, was abandoned after 1897 when the military bought the Mount Austin Hotel.
[5] HK Hansard for 28 September 1933
[6] Blue Books and Estimates for 1933/1934
[7] HK Hansard for 27 September 1934
[8] Administrative Report for 1939
[9] *South China Morning Post,* 13 June 1941
[10] 'Chater collection' file. See note [1]

10 The house Fujimura built (1942–45)
[1] *Hongkong News,* 22 February 1942
[2] Government House plans
[3] Respectively, Hidejiro Kajiya (Kyoto) and Kanebo Decorator (Osaka)
[4] *Hongkong holiday,* Emily Hahn. Doubleday, New York, 1946
[5] 'Chapter collection' file. See Chapter 9, note [1]. The slashed royal portraits are still at Government House.
[6] *Hongkong News,* 21 February 1943
[7] *Hongkong News,* 23 July 1943

11 Reoccupation (1945–46)
[1] Today's Victoria District Court. See chapter 1, note [6].
[2] *Althea. Darlings, I've had a ball!,* as told to Trish Sheppard. Ure Smith, Sydney, 1975
[3] 'Civil affairs 1945' files, HKRS 170, D 1. Nos. 41 and 43 Repulse Bay Road were 'Monte Verde' and 'Twin Brook', now apartment blocks of the same names.
[4] 'Mountain Lodge' file, BL 13/641/46. The gate-lodge is still there. So are the foundations of the main house, covered by a Chinese pavilion. The flat lawn immediately below, to the south, is the site of the original military sanatorium/Mountain Lodge (Mark I) and of the Mountain Lodge (Mark II) that replaced it. The entire grounds are now a public park.
[5] 'Magazine Gap area' file, BL 12/631/46
[6] 'Fanling Lodge' file, BL 2/631/46
[7] 'Government House' file, BL 3/2131/46

12 Since 1946
[1] *China Mail/South China Morning Post,* 16 April 1947
[2] *South China Morning Post,* 4 June 1950. The editor was Henry Ching.
[3] 'Chater collection' file. See chapter 9, note [1].
[4] *Via ports, from Hong Kong to Hong Kong,* Sir Alexander Grantham. Hong Kong University Press, 1965
[5] HK Hansard for 21/28 March 1956
[6] *South China Morning Post,* 30 March 1956
[7] *China Mail,* 29 March 1956
[8] Partly occupied today by Mansfield Road government quarters

Sources

Government:
Hong Kong Blue Books
Hong Kong Administrative/Annual Reports
Hong Kong Government Gazettes
Hong Kong Sessional Papers
Hong Kong Hansard
Hong Kong Government Archives (see Notes)
United Kingdom Government Archives (see Notes)

Newspapers:

Canton Register
Chinese Repository
Friend of China
Hong Kong Register
China Mail
Dixon's Hong Kong Recorder

Hong Kong Daily Press
Hongkong Telegraph
South China Morning Post
Hongkong News
Illustrated London News

Books:
Narrative of a voyage round the world, performed in HMS Sulphur, Sir Edward Belcher. London, 1843
Narrative of the voyages and services of the Nemesis, W. D. Bernard and W. H. Hall. London, 1844
An ADC's recollections of service in China, Arthur Cunynghame. London, 1844
The Chinese war: an account of all the operations of the British forces, J. Ouchterlony. London, 1844
Wanderings in China, Robert Fortune. London, 1847
Statements and suggestions regarding Hong Kong addressed to the Hon. Francis Scott, MP. London, 1850/51
China: being 'The Times' special correspondence from China in the years 1857–58, G. Wingrove Cooke. London, 1858
To China and back, being a diary kept out and home, Albert Smith. London (privately), 1859
The treaty ports of China and Japan, Mayers, Dennys and King. Hong Kong, 1867
Visit of His Royal Highness the Duke of Edinburgh, Rev. William Beach. Hong Kong, 1869
Hong Kong almanack, 1885
Wanderings in China, C. F. Gordon Cumming. Edinburgh, 1886
The cruise of HMS Bacchante 1879–1882, compiled from the private journals, letters and note-books of Prince Albert Victor and Prince George of Wales with additions by John N. Dalton. London, 1886
The Duke and Duchess of Connaught. A brief account of the visit of Their Royal Highnesses to Hong Kong in 1890. Hong Kong, 1890
Handbook to Hong Kong. Hong Kong, 1893
Index to the streets, houses and leased lots of Victoria, Victoria Peak and Kowloon. Hong Kong, 1894
Europe in China. The history of Hong Kong from the beginning to the year 1882. E. J. Eitel. Hong Kong, 1895
The history of the laws and courts of Hong Kong, J. W. Norton-Kyshe. London, 1898
My colonial service in British Guiana, etc., Sir William Des Voeux. London, 1903
Twentieth century impressions of Hong Kong, Shanghai and other Treaty Ports. London, 1908
The Chater collection. Pictures relating to China, Hong Kong, Macao, 1655–1860, James Orange. London, 1924
Picturesque Hong Kong and its dependencies, R. C. Hurley. Hong Kong, 1925
Hong Kong. Birth, adolescence and coming of age, G. R. Sayer. Oxford, 1937
Hong Kong incident, P. Harrop. London, 1942
Hong Kong under Japanese occupation. A case study of the enemy's technique of control, Robert Ward. Washington, 1943
Operations in the Far East from 17 October 1940 to 27 December 1941, Air

Chief Marshall Sir Robert Brooke-Popham. London, 1948
The diocese of Victoria, Hong Kong, G. B. Endacott and D. E. She. Hong Kong, 1949
A history of Hong Kong, G. B. Endacott, London, 1958
Lugard, Marjery Perham. London, 1960
A biographical sketch-book of early Hong Kong, G. B. Endacott. Singapore, 1962
Verandah, James Pope-Hennessy. London, 1964
Via ports, from Hong Kong to Hong Kong, Sir Alexander Grantham. Hong Kong, 1965
The hidden years, John Luff. Hong Kong, 1967
Hong Kong's first Government House, Dafydd Evans. Hong Kong Royal Asiatic Society paper, 1968
Colony in conflict, John Cooper. Hong Kong, 1970
Palaces of the Raj, Mark Bence-Jones. London, 1973
Hong Kong 1862–1919, G. R. Sayer. Hong Kong, 1975
Footprints, Sir Selwyn Selwyn-Clarke. Hong Kong, 1975

Illustration:
Front endpaper: Plan of the City of Victoria, 1889 (detail). HKRS 207, D&S 12&2. Public Records Officer, Hong Kong
Frontispiece: Drawings by R. J. Johnson
Page 4: Oil-painting of Hong Kong Harbour (detail), 1850s, by unknown artist, Museum of Art, Hong Kong
Page 7: Engraving. Museum of Art.
Page 9: Photograph of sepia wash drawing by E. Ashworth, 1845, Museum of Art
Page 11: Plan dated December 1843. Vol. 2, CO 129. Public Record Office, London
Page 13: *Illustrated London News,* 27 December 1856
Page 15: *Illustrated London News,* 11 April 1857
Page 17: See 'Notes', chapter 2
Page 21: 'View of Spring Gardens, 20th August 1846' (detail), Bruce/Maclure lithograph, Museum of Art
Pages 25, 26, 27: See 'Notes', chapter 4
Page 32: Water-colour attributed to M.A. Baptista, Museum of Art
Page 35: *Dixon's Hong Kong Recorder,* 6 May 1859
Page 36: Photograph from 1859–64 collection of the 5th Duke of Newcastle, held by University of Nottingham, reproduced by courtesy of the present Duke
Page 38: 'The Grand Harbour Hongkong', c. 1860. Water-colour by R. Shannon. Museum of Art
Pages 40, 41, 45, 46, 50, 58, 59, 62, 63, 65, 67, 71, 73, 74, 93, 94: Museum of History, Hong Kong
Page 43: Oil painting of Hong Kong from the Harbour, 1860s. Reproduced by courtesy of Jardine, Matheson & Co. Ltd.
Page 52: *Illustrated London News,* 10 January 1885
Page 55: Oil painting, Museum of Art
Page 70: Reproduced by courtesy of the owner, Major-General Sir Robert Neville
Pages 75 and 77: Reproduced by courtesy of the owner, Wm. A. Stewart
Pages 86, 96, 98, 101, 103, 105, 106. Government Information Services, Hong Kong
Pages 83 and 90: Reproduced by courtesy of Kinya Nakao
Pages 84 and 85: Architectural Office, PWD, Hong Kong
Page 89: Reproduced by courtesy of Hongkong and Shanghai Hotels
Page 97: China Mail, 2 May 1946